The *Original*
THE INCREDIBLE
POTATO

A COOKBOOK AND HISTORY
Revised Edition

Over 200 Distinctive International Recipes
PLUS Health Notes, History and Scientific Potato Lore

Acknowledgement

Many thanks to all the people who helped with this book, especially my husband, Paul, who encouraged me when the going was rough; to Ron Loewen whose interest in good nutrition prompted mine; my editor, Margo Embury, who guided when it was needed and Nancy Millar for believing in the project.

Enjoy a good health!

BY AGNES TOEWS-ANDREWS

Agnes T. Andrews

front cover photograph
Mussel and Potato Salad II, page 58

The *Original* The Incredible Potato
A Cookbook and History
By Agnes Toews Andrews

Revised Edition – April 2000

Canadian Cataloguing in Publication Data

Toews-Andrews, Agnes, 1948-
   The original the incredible potato – a cookbook and history

   Includes index.
   ISBN: 0-9686765-2-9

1. Cookery (Potatoes) I. Title: II. Title: The incredible potato.
TX803.P8T63 2000   641.6'521   C00-910349-X

Front Cover Photography: **Patricia Holdsworth**
Patricia Holdsworth Photography
Regina, Saskatchewan

Back Cover Photography: **Paul Andrews**
Beaverlodge, Alta, Canada

Preface Photography: **Anthony Wing**
Visual Events Photography, Delta BC, Canada

Designed, Printed and Produced in Canada by:
Centax Books, a Division of PrintWest Communications
Publishing Director, Photo Designer & Food Stylist: Margo Embury
Designer: Blair Fraser
1150 Eighth Avenue, Regina, Saskatchewan, Canada S4R 1C9
(306) 525-2304   FAX: (306) 757-2439
E-mail: centax@printwest.com   www.centaxbooks.com

Table of Contents

Preface

More than a decade has gone by since I researched the potato. I am still rediscovering the endless possibilities of this highly nutritious edible tuber, of the family Solanum Tuberosum. It is my pleasure to add to this potato collection several personal, historical notes of significant importance.

In 1995, exactly 10 years after *The Incredible Potato – A Cookbook and History* was first published, I received word that I had cancer of the ovaries. Before I began a strict Macrobiotic healing diet, I used a cleansing, toning, rebalancing diet that consisted of: watermelon, whole organic spelt wheat, wild greens, and POTATOES.

Watermelon is high in oxygen and hydrogen, a naturally distilled water that quickly nourishes the cells. Whole spelt wheat gave me stamina and B vitamins; the wild greens are high in chlorophyll, they cleanse the blood and remove environmental toxins. The POTATO is a nightshade plant, ruled by the moon. It strengthens and heals the sexual organs in humans. The sexual organs in humans are also governed by the moon.

The amazing antioxidant-coenzyme called Alpha Lipic Acid is found in abundance in potatoes. This natural acid that the body manufactures is depleted in the body by tobacco smoke, alcohol and other harmful and free radical forming substances. When in abundance in the body, it protects us from creating cancer cells as well as preventing capillary bruising and aging (Beth Ley, 1996).

The potato is high in ENERGY: niacin-Vitamin B6, thiamine-B1, riboflavin-B2, Vitamin A, Vitamin C. When boiling unpeeled potatoes there is little or no vitamin C loss; one potato provides a day's supply of Vitamin C. (Ora Smith, *Potatoes: Production, Storing, Processing*). The potato is important nutritionally as a source of protein. The nutritional or biological protein in potatoes is extraordinarily high (Schupan, 1959). When compared to wheat, potatoes contain substantially more of all the essential amino acids, except histidine (Hughes, 1958). The potato is high in nitrogen. The coefficient of digestibility of nitrogen is about 76 in the intact potato, and 83 in the pressed juice. The protein efficiency rates of cooked potatoes and potato flour proteins are the same (Cloudhuri, 1963). A MacGillivay and Bosley study (1962) indicates that potatoes produce more essential amino acids per acre than oats, beef or lamb.

Shortly before I knew that I had cancer of the ovaries, while relaxing in my hot tub one late March evening, I was looking out at my front lawn. I saw a new circular garden blossoming with a "white flowered" plant. When a friend called and asked if she could gift me with a variety of heritage potatoes, I immediately knew that the garden I had envisioned was to be a potato garden. The reason for the potato garden remained a mystery until mid-May, when I pushed a shovel forcefully into the ground, hit a large stone, and "burst" something inside my lower body. The cancerous cysts on my ovaries had burst and spread poison throughout my stomach and intestinal wall. I was in a healing crisis such as I had never experienced before! Because both of my parents had died of cancer, and cancer of the uterus and ovaries was considered genetic in my mother's family, I had surmised that at some point in my life I would have to deal with the disease.

The story of healing my cancer and other challenges is to be published in *Clearing Karma—From Jerusalem to Little Fort* ISBN: 0-9686765-0-2. A second book: *Healing: for Today, Tomorrow, and Always* (Isis Moon Publishing) is also forthcoming.

I stayed on a simple diet of watermelon, wheat, greens and potatoes for 6 weeks. I baked the potatoes and made potato juice which I drank raw. After this, I began a healing Macrobiotic diet. Macrobiotic means "All Encompassing, Abundant Life Cooking" and is an ancient traditional system of "healing with foods". One takes into consideration: the cooking method and how it affects the body; using different foods for the seasons and climate; how certain foods heal our organs. One tries as much as possible to eat locally grown organic foods, including those that grow in a similar climate, and also sea vegetables and miso soups. This is a simplistic definition of Macrobiotic cooking. There are many good books written on the subject.

Within four months I had healed myself of cancer of the ovaries, breasts, and uterus without surgery, radiation or chemotherapy. By the end of September I had regained my energy and well being. A positive mind set and working with hands-on healing—Reiki—also facilitated me at this time.

The potato is an alkaline tuber of world importance. The natives of Peru eat rice and vegetables as well as potatoes. The potato originated on the Isle of Chiloe, off the coast of Peru, where it is still a staple. Its importance as a world food crop cannot be underestimated. Peruvians invariably cook potatoes in their skins as this cooking method retains the nutrients and FLAVOUR of the potato.

The solanine level in most potatoes is about 90 parts per million, which is about one-quarter of the danger level determined by researchers (Steve Gagne in *The Energetics of Food*). Studies have shown that people with rheumatoid arthritis have shown improvement when following a good diet; eliminating meat, chicken and the nightshades: sweet peppers, eggplant, tomatoes, and potatoes, for a time.

Steve Gagne also tells us that the potato is a supportive food for excess heat and dryness in the body system. Cornelia Aihara and Herman Aihara (*Natural Healing from Head to Toe*) use potato concentrate as a remedy for stomach or duodenal ulcers. Macrobiotic consultants, the Aiharas tell us that potatoes are "salt-suckers" and can be very helpful in reducing sodium in tissues of people who have consumed far too much bad salt (refined salt with added iodine).

When the Spanish first encountered potatoes they observed the Indians in Peru soaking the potatoes in water and then letting them freeze in the cold mountain air. Then they dried them in the sun and proceeded to rub off the skins by walking on them with their bare feet. The potatoes turned black and were soaked in water for 3 days before being dried for storage, to be used in soups or ground into flour to make bread. This is still how chuno is prepared in Peru. It is the way to preserve potatoes for long-term storage and has been used in Peru for over 2000 years. It's the ancient Incan method for preserving potatoes (Robert Rhoades,1982).

In ancient times and now, herbalists and wild foragers pay tribute to the foods and herbs that they gather, by offering prayers. An ancient Anazazi prayer before eating was an acknowledgement of their food: "I honor the life that thou hast given me to be fed, I am grateful for the sacrifice thou hast given for me, my spirit bows to your spirit, and I shall waste no part of you." In ancient times we offered libations to the potato spirits, made pottery in honor of them, and held the POTATO in high esteem.

All organisms, animate and inanimate: minerals, plants, animals, humans upon Earth apparently have an overlighting nature spirit (Machelle Small Wright *Behaving as Though all Life on Earth Mattered* & Barbara Hand Clow *Heart of The Christos*). Incas especially honoured the potato because the wellness of their people depended on this most important of foods. It enhances the sexual prowess of men and women. Incas believed their fruitfulness depended largely on the potato! The Irish have proven this in recent times. The potato enhances, heals and keeps the sexual organs in the male and female strong. I think we can conceivably deduce that when the sexual organs are strong, sexual desire in both men and women increases, which is why the English thought the potato to be an aphrodisiac. In the 16th century the Incas extended 2,600 miles throughout South America. The potato and other staples such as corn, beans, quinoa, fish and sea vegetables were their main diet.

A perfect macrobiotic diet! I write about my various karmic connections to the potato in the book *Clearing Karma From Jerusalem To Little Fort*.

I have included in the revised, *THE Original INCREDIBLE POTATO—A COOKBOOK AND HISTORY*, new information on Organic Potato Seed and Heritage Potatoes along with addresses of suppliers. I feel that it is highly important to keep a supply of genetically unaltered potatoes and other foods at this time of experimentation. Also, to be able to grow organic high-quality potatoes, in our back yards or in pots on our apartment balconies (as they do in Israel), is such a rewarding pleasure, that I know all sensible people will be doing so, since our planet is in an emergency situation. What we need most of all are foods that are high in antioxidants, to clear our bodies of all the chemicals that we have ingested.

I have added new potato recipes to this collection of international potato cookery from my travels throughout the Mediterranean and Caribbean. Nowadays I try to use only organically grown food and garden produce.

While living in the Mediterranean area I enjoyed potatoes smothered in olive oil from the first press of olives in Lebanon, and potatoes organically grown in the Nile River district in Egypt, exquisitely served with green beans and cilantro. Traversing the Greek islands I indulged in local feta cheese and potato dishes. In Israel, of course, I sampled potato latkes and potato maraska many times, recipes which are already in this book. I have written about my travels in the Mediterranean area, about food, cooking and customs in the book titled, *Garbage and Flowers—My Year's Sojourn in the Holy Land*. ISBN: 1-55056-536-2 (Isis Moon Publishing). It is a highly descriptive, travelogue created from my journals while living in the Mediterranean area.

I have, over the years, received many recipes from potato afficionados from all over the world. Thank you for those! My favourite potatoes are still fresh new potatoes, dug in mid-summer, steamed and served with a good pinch of Celtic sea salt, garlic, parsley and dill, or enhanced with organic olive oil and fresh lemon juice.

I still have a beautiful circular garden of potatoes; although smaller than that of the year of '95. Its centre has several corn plants. Together these plants create a special garden for me. I honor it greatly.

I hold the potato in high esteem and have great regard for this most nutritious of foods.

"Long live *The Incredible Potato*"

Foreword

According to authorities, man did not migrate to the Americas until somewhere between 20,000 - 10,000 B.C. By about 7,000 B.C., the retreat of the glaciers and sudden changes in temperature, resulted in the depredation of man and beast.

6,000 years before Christ, a wild vegetable was being gathered by nomadic Indians on a 12,000 foot plateau, in the Andes. I wonder if the Incas, who were enthralled with gold and silver, realized the wealth beneath their feet!

The Incas in the 16th Century called it the papa, the Indian name for sweet potato was thought to be batata. From these two words emerged the English word, POTATO.

I have researched the potato with a passion. This vegetable literally conquered the world! The potato is a gem in all aspects. The "KING" is fat-free, extremely high in minerals and vitamins, and high in roughage. If continuing recessions develop into a full-fledged depression, remember that potatoes, dressed with a little margarine sustained a Scandinavian man healthily for 300 days! About 23 medium potatoes equal 2,500 calories, which is the approximate daily adult requirement. The more I found out about the potato, the more fascinated I became. Nouvelle cuisine gourmet magazines, antiquated cookbooks, magazine articles, friends' cookbooks, restaurants and libraries, all became potato haunts. The potato held me captive.

A great deal of information was gleaned from the research conducted by Robert E. Rhoades, for National Geographic. Research led to further research. As I lay in my bed in North Bay, Ontario, I dreamed about potatoes. The importance of good nutrition, the state of our economy, and the inspiration of a keen interest in anthropology, prompted me to re-explore the potato. The result is "The Incredible Potato Cookbook and History".

Growing up in the Fraser Valley, potatoes were standard fare at our house. I remember my parents planting potatoes, then spending relatively little time with them, except for the occasional dusting for blight or pests (the Fraser Valley is known to be lush and wet), until the plentiful harvest in late August. The large brown potatoes were stored in brown gunny sacks in the root cellar. When March rolled around and warmed things up a little, the eyes on our potatoes would sprout, and the potatoes became soft and shriveled up. That was when my favorite potato dishes would appear, such as scalloped potatoes and diced potatoes smothered in sour cream and onions. Potatoes are 99% fat free, can a little sour cream be so bad!!

Somehow the potato seemed unsophisticated and not fashionable when I began to cook, I substituted rice and pastas for potatoes and do you know that none of these substitutes come near to being as complete a food as potatoes? Did you know that, during both world wars in Europe, it was proven that malnutrition could be avoided by a diet consisting entirely of potatoes? Research indicated a unique, phenomenal vegetable with approximately eight species and thousands of varieties.

The potato is rich in easily digested carbohydrates, chiefly starch. It is a fair source of protein, a good source of phosphorous, potassium and iron; high in Vitamin C. It is also an important source of B vitamins. Compared to pasta and rice, potatoes have more than double the amount of minerals and vitamins.

In this book, I take pride in presenting to you a wide range of recipes. Most are simple, cost and calorie conscious. Some are more exotic but entirely possible! Many of the recipes that I looked at were enticing but too overburdened with fat. The recipes which were laden with fats and calories have been revamped and updated, using chicken stock base, and they do not require butter for good taste.

Overall timing includes paring, dicing, cooking. There are some calorie counts, and estimated numbers of servings. I have found that adding a few potatoes to most of the given recipes can be done when stretching is necessary.

I appreciate the time-saving element in baking potatoes in the microwave. Four potatoes take as little as 10-18 minutes. But, if you try to bake wet potatoes in the microwave, the center of the potato tends to turn gummy. I am not a microwave potato fan. The texture and taste of a potato when baked in a conventional, convection or broiler oven is much better than when the potato is baked in a microwave oven. Steaming is the best method for cooking potatoes, to retain nutrients although it is inconvenient if you are cooking a large amount. Baking is the next best method.

Boiling potatoes is next best to baking. Always boil gently, with as little water as possible. Add a few grains of salt, if you wish. The water that the potatoes are steamed in is extremely high in vitamins and minerals. Don't throw it out! Provided you have not overcooked the potatoes, and steamed off all of the goodness, this water may be used to enhance soups, stews, sauces, breads or vegetable cocktails.

Potatoes are making history at our house. Hardly a meal goes by without the inclusion of the pomme de terre. The potatoes' past history is dispersed throughout the book. People and potatoes! Read and relish!

Pass on the legend of the potato, teach your children about its nutrition and make the potato high art. Employ the POTATO, apple of the earth, at every fine meal. "GUTEN APPETIT"

Growing Garden Potatoes

The potato is an annual plant, botanically related to the tomato, pepper, and eggplant. The edible part, or tuber, is anatomically an enlarged part of the stem developing underground. Since plants grown from seeds of the potato fruit do not produce true to type, the potato is mainly propagated from tubers. Although seeds are now available for trial in home gardens.

The potato is highly adapted to most growing conditions of Canada and the United States. Higher temperatures suppress tuber formation.

Tubers begin to form about 40-50 days after planting, coinciding approximately with, but not related to, the onset of flowering.

It takes 90-140 days from planting date for potatoes to reach maturity, depending on location and variety.

There are some 50 varieties licensed for sale in Canada, but only a few are grown extensively in one area. Varieties are classified as early, mid-season, or late.

The use of good planting stock is essential to obtain a satisfactory crop of potatoes. Always try to obtain potato stocks specially grown for planting, that is, those certified and inspected. They may cost a little more, but their use may prevent failures and promotion of disease.

Planting

Stock potatoes are usually cut in two, four, or six chunky pieces depending on the size of the tuber. Each piece should have at least one or two eyes and weigh approximately 1¾ oz. (50 g). Curing the potato pieces in a relatively warm, damp, place for one-three weeks before planting, encourages rapid healing of cut surfaces, increases resistance to decay, and favors sprouting.

Potatoes of the best quality with a high dry-matter content, and good texture are usually grown on heavy soils, which are predominatly mineral in composition rather than organic. Potatoes do not grow well in poorly drained or waterlogged soils. Drainage must be good. Since the potato is a fairly heavy feeder, nutrients from organic matter alone usually are not sufficient to meet its needs. To avoid mineral deficiency, supplement the soil with 5-10-10; 6-12-12; or 5-20-20. First number pertains to nitrogen, second, phosphorus, third, potash.

Usually the potato is planted in May, about two weeks before the last killing frost is expected. At planting time, make holes or furrows about 6" (13 cm) deep with a trowel or hoe. For most garden soils, apply 1½ tablespoons (22 mL) of complete fertilizer at the bottom of each hole. Cover with 1" (2.5 cm) of soil, put in stock pieces, top with soil to ground level. Do not allow stock pieces to come in direct contact with the concentrated fertilizer.

Plant stock pieces 10-12" (25-30 cm) apart, in rows about 31½" (80 cm) apart. Planting should be slightly shallower in heavy soils.

Do not allow weeds to build up. Start hoeing early, when weeds are just germinating; one good hoeing also aerates the soil, loosens the surface, and allows better absorption and retention of soil moisture.

When hoeing, mound a little hill of soil around the base of the plant. This extra soil stifles small weeds, prevents greening or sun-burning of any tubers, and protects them from damage against frosts which occur in the fall.

Lack of moisture is said to be the main cause of reduced potato yield. Cycles of hot dry weather, followed by heavy rains prompting sudden periods of rapid growth, are the causes of rough, knobby, malformed or cracked tubers. Supplement low rainfall periods with watering from a garden hose, as adequate watering, especially during the period of tuber formation and enlargement, is essential for good tuber growth.

Controlling Pests and Diseases

The potato is susceptible to numerous diseases, among which potato scab and late blight are probably the most persistent and troublesome across the country. Scab causes blemishes but usually does not destroy the usefulness of the rest of the potato.

Growing potatoes year after year in the same part of the garden encourages a buildup of diseases and insect pests, which can be handled by rotating your potato plantings to other areas of your garden. Good control of diseases and pests of potatoes can be obtained in the garden by a specially prepared home garden spray or by dust mixtures. Various formulations are available under brand names with directions for use.

Potato diseases, insect pest damages, other disorders and their control measures are available from your nearest agricultural representative or government specialist.

Harvesting and Storage

Harvest before a killing frost. Potatoes reach full maturity when the tops of the plants become withered. Although tubers of acceptable size may be harvested at any time for immediate use, if you plan to store them for prolonged periods it is best to defer digging them until after the crop matures. Well-matured tubers have firm, hardened skin, are less susceptible to injuries, and store better than immature tubers. Where the growing season is too short to mature late varieties, tops can be prematurely killed simply by cutting them off when tubers have reached acceptable size. The skin will harden sufficiently if tubers are allowed to remain in the soil, about 10 days before harvesting.

A 20 foot (6 m) row of potatoes, should yield 20-35 lbs. (9-15 kg) of tubers. Be gentle with tubers. Dig them up carefully with a spade and carry them in padded boxes or cardboard containers.

Do not expose tubers unnecessarily to sunlight. After digging, allow them to dry in a shaded area in the open, but not for more than a few hours, or in your basement. Drying helps to harden the skin. Avoid digging on a wet day, since wet soil tends to stick to tubers and is a good reservoir for rotting organisms.

The potato is a living plant mass that continues to age until cooked. A mature tuber at harvest has a natural rest period of two to three months, depending on variety, during which time its sprouts are dormant, and will not grow under normal conditions. With proper storage, the tubers can be extended for up to six months. Late varieties have a longer rest period and usually store much better than early varieties.

Ideally, table potatoes store best at 38-45°F (4-7°C). This temperature is low enough to prevent sprouting and shrinkage, but not too low to cause excessive sweetening. Certain sugars tend to accumulate in tubers kept at low temperatures. Try to keep your tubers in relatively warm and humid conditions during the first 2-3 weeks of storage, as this promotes healing of wounds and cuts and increases storageability.

Agnes in her Twelve-Spoke Potato Wheel Garden

Potato Varieties and Usages

For an update on popular home garden potato varieties I contacted Clive Schaupmeyer, MSc, in Taber Alberta; Beckers, a potato seed company in Trout Creek, Ontario; and Seeds of Diversity, an Oregon based Organic Heritage Seed Supplier. Clive, a potato agronomist, filled me in on what's happening in Canada, with comments on several varieties of potatoes. His comments and Becker's ten most popular varieties for home gardens are listed on page 1.

Canadian Sources For Specialty Potatoes

- T&T Seeds – Box 1710, Winnipeg, Manitoba, MBR 3P6
- McFadden Seed Co. – 30-9th St. Suite 200, Brandon, Man. R7A 6N4
- Beckers seeds – RR#1 Trout Creek, Ontario, P0H 2L0
- Vesey's Seeds Ltd – York, PEI C0A 1P0
- Lindenberg Seeds – 803 Princess Ave. Brandon Manitoba, R7A 0P5
- Alberta Nurseries and Seeds – Box 20, Bowden Alberta, T0m 0K0
- Allen, Ken – 536 MacDowell St, Kingston, Ontario K7K 4W7
- Brickmans – RR#1 Sebringville, Ontario, N0K 1X0
- Dacha Brinka – 45232 Strathcona Rd. Chilliwack, BC V2P 3T2
- Blueberry Hill Farms – Fort St. John, BC. V1J 4H9
- Farm Gate Seed Potatoes – Box 123, Summerside, PEI. C1N 4P6
- Potato News: www.potatonews.com

USA and UK Potato Specialty Suppliers

- Abundant Life Seed Foundation, Box 772, Port Townsend, Washington 38368
- Bountiful Gardens, 18001 Shafer Ranch Road, Willits California 95490- (Organically grown seeds)
- Chiltern Seeds, Bortee Stile, Ulverstone Cumbrei, England, IA127PB
- Seeds of Change: (organic) Box 15700, Santa Fe, NM. USA 87506-5700

International Organic Potato Information
"Seeds of Change" Potato Varieties

"Seeds of Change" farms in Oregon and New Mexico incorporate science and serendipity on their research farms. It's "eat your way through" as Howard-Yana Shapiro, PhD. puts it. Shapiro, their director of agriculture, likes to ask visitors to sample the flavour and appeal of different vegetable varieties. Unlike other plant breeding programs which work toward uniform fruits and vegetables, easy to machine harvest and ship, nutrition is the primary consideration of their research and this determines which of their successful hybrids to pursue further. On their 100% organically grown seed farms, Seeds of Change furthers awareness of sustainable agriculture and socially responsible food production systems. Their potato varieties are as follows: All-Blue, Purple Viking, Alaskan Sweetheart, Norland, Desiree, Gladstone, Red Sangre, Chipeta, German Butterball, Russet Nugget, Yellow Finn & Yukon Gold. "Our goal," states Alan Kapular, PhD, "is to provide the backyard gardener with tools for their own health and nutrition." From potatoes to corn, carrots and onions, Seeds of Change research is working toward this goal by developing new varieties and examining older heritage plants. Over one-third of their seeds are heritage and traditional varieties.

Canadian Organic Growers (COG), founded in 1975, is a national information and networking organization for organic farmers, gardeners and consumers. Other important organic organizations are: the International Federation of Organic Agricultural Movements (IFOAM); Certified Organic Association of BC (COABC); the Organic Trade Association (OTA); and Ecological Agriculture Projects, "Seeds of Diversity" Box 36, Station A, Toronto, Ontario, Canada M4T 2C7 and "Inforganics" Jeff Johnston, PO Box 95, Riverport, Nova Scotia. B0J 2W0.

BC is one of the fastest growing organic agricultural sectors in Canada, with increasing numbers of producers and a high consumer awareness. Organically grown potatoes—with a high use of nitrogen matter—can contain as much as four times the amount of vitamins and minerals as potatoes grown with chemical fertilizer.

An American organic potato seed producer in Maine is WOOD-PRAIRIE FARM, Maine, USA. The e-mail address is: info@Shop-Maine.com. They offer three select potatoes to "satisfy the most discriminating palate": Yukon Gold, All-Blue and Rose Gold.

There are many other organic seed potato sources in North America. Information about potatoes and organic seed potatoes can be obtained on the internet at: www.agrisurf.com.

Federation of Organic Agricultural Movements, Genetic Engineering, Irradiation

IFOAM(International Organic Agricultural Movements) is committed to promoting organic agriculture as a sound, sustainable alternative to current intensive farming practices. It is urging member organizations throughout the world to campaign on a national and local level to help achieve this objective. IFOAM has 740 member organizations and associates in over 100 countries, representing all components of organic agriculture, farmers, certifiers, processors, retailers and researchers. IFOAM has scientific conferences every two years.

Genetic engineering emerged as a major theme, during the 1998 Plata del Mar conference, as one of the greatest threats to human, environmental and global health in the history of agriculture. A petition launched at the conference, calling for a ban, will be used to bring pressure on regulatory agencies and governments worldwide. The international organic movement is determined to uphold the right of all consumers to have access to food free of all contamination by genetically modified organisms (GMOs), but is confronted by a growing threat of genetic pollution resulting from production of GM crops. It is estimated that world-wide production of GM crops in 1998 has reached over 40 million hectares. However, IFOAM believes that concerted international action mobilizing public opposition to genetic engineering could reverse the commercial introduction of GM crops, now seen by many governments as inevitable.

Canada and the US have approved genetically engineered potatoes, and they are not labelled. Ask if your food store has a policy about genetically engineered potatoes. For further information contact:

Bernard Geier, IFOAM Head Office, Germany. Tel + 49 6853 5190; fax: 49 6853 30110 email: ifoam@-online.de.

Shalinova (1966) found that irradiation of potatoes soon after harvest causes considerable loss of vitamin C, while irradiation a month or later after harvest causes little loss.

International Potato Trivia

New Brunswick grows a lot of Canada's potatoes. They even have a provincial holiday to gather potatoes! The last two weeks in September are school holidays when youngsters help harvest on the family potato farms. After the "rouging' is completed (picking off bugs and checking for potato diseases in July), the harvesting of the year's crop begins. The children dig and gather the potatoes while the teenagers drive the machinery and sort potatoes.

New Brunswick is home to McCain's, a large potato processor. They make local potatoes into frozen products: french fries, hash browns, curls, etc. Commercial deep-fried potatoes lose only 18% of nutrients and very little Vitamin C (Krylova, 1957). Dr. Warren K. Coleman, a plant physiologist at the Potato Research Centre in Fredericton, reports that the Yukon Gold is still an important table variety while Shepody is a globally important french fry variety. Both were developed in Canada (1980). The New Brunswick Potato Agency can be reached at: PO Box 238, Florenceville, NB, Canada, E0J 1K0.

MacDonald's restaurant food chain's potato patches are in Idaho. The Idaho State Potato Growers announced a new variety in August 1999, named "Russet Bannock". It has improved flavor and storage. Scotland's Potato Lady, Margaret McLean, grows more than 200 varieties on her farm in Perthshire, Scotland. She plants the collection on 1½ acres, carrying on the work of her late husband who was an ardent collector of rare potatoes. She has purple and red potatoes called Purple Congo and Beetroot. Most of her varieties come from the British Isles, Holland, and Scandinavia. They include the Shetland Black, which is black skinned with grey flesh. Margaret says she runs the collection as a hobby rather than a business, nevertheless it stands as an important continuation toward preserving the genetic diversity of the potato. In addition to maintaining the living potato museum Margaret grows 20 acres of commercial potatoes.

Prince Edward Island, Canada's smallest province, annually produces more than 30% of the total Canadian potato crop. In 1998, 640 producers grew 43,600 hectares of potatoes including 11,246 hectares of potatoes for seed. The first record of potato production in PEI comes from a 1771 report sent by the then Colonial Governor to England. He described the crop as "phenomenal" and by 1790 seed was being exported to the neighbouring colonies and by 1830 to the West Indies. Production and export of "Certified" seed potatoes commenced 82 years ago.Currently more than 30 varieties of potatoes are grown to supply customers in North and South America, Europe, the Middle East and Africa.

Popular, Specialty & Heritage Varieties
Canadian, American & European

RUSSET BURBANK (1874)
- dry, white
- very good for baking
- mid to late season

NORLAND
- moist, red skin, white flesh
- good boiling qualities, early

RED PONTIAC (1954)
- boiling, baking, moist
- red skin, white flesh, mid season

WARBA (1933)
- all purpose, dry, white flesh
- best eaten fresh, early

ERAMOSA
- smooth, round, white
- all purpose, "the earliest"

RED VIKING
- popular home variety
- moist, red, for boiling
- mid season, good flavour

BATOCHE
- red, waxy, mostly for boiling
- mid season

ALASKA SWEETHEART
- pink flesh, red skin
- boiling, late season

YUKON GOLD (1980)
- popular, yellow fleshed, dry
- good flavour, early

IRISH COBBLER (LATE 1800s)
- excellent boiling and baking, round
- excellent flavour, white, early

GREEN MOUNTAIN (1885)
- netted, long, dry tuber
- firm, boiling, distinct flavour, late

SAXON
- white skin, creamy flesh
- baking, boiling, mid-season
- excellent flavour

GERMAN FINGER
- a fingerling, boiling, French fries
- firm, yellow flesh, dense, tasty
- late season

CHIEFTAIN
- red skin, white flesh, boiling,
- late

SHEPODY
- white, baking/boiling/French fry
- long, late season

BANANA
- yellow, firm, waxy fingerling
- good flavour, soups/stews, very late

ALL BLUE
- deep blue skin, lavender flesh
- good flavour, late season

CHEROKEE (1954)
- white skin & flesh, flat round tuber, adapted to clay soils
- boiling, late season

PURPLE VIKING
- pretty spud, white flesh, purple skin
- boiling, mid season

DESIREE (1962)
- red skin, golden flesh
- boiling, firm, distinct flavour, late

GLADSTONE
- red flesh, yellow skin, baker, boiler
- mid-season

YELLOW FINN
- yellow flesh and skin
- very tasty, buttery, sweet flavoured
- mid season, high yields

ISLAND SUNSHINE (PEI) (1999)
- baking, boiling, late
- excellent flavour, bright yellow flesh

1

Tips on Buying Potatoes

— Buy according to grade
— The best quality is firm, well-shaped, cut free, and free from blemishes and decay
— Buy the size best suited to your needs
— Buy only amounts which can be stored in a cool spot, as they spoil and become soft quickly in warm temperatures. Best storing temperature is 38-45°F(2-8°C)
— Some varities are for fresh use only, use up in two-three weeks
— Potatoes loose their sugar and become starchier with age
— Avoid buying "green" potatoes, as the tubers have been exposed to light during growth and the presence of these greening compounds (gly-coalkaloids), if eaten in large quantities, may cause stomach upsets. There should be no danger of poisoning from these potatoes, if the green areas are removed.

Storing Potatoes from the Store

— Do not freeze potatoes, they become watery
— Store in a cool place, where air can circulate
— Never store in a plastic bag, potatoes must be able to breathe or they will rot
— Store in a dark place, as light causes potatoes to acquire a bitter taste
— Bruised or cracked potatoes should be used immediately, as they lose vitamins and starch if stored too long
— If stored properly, potatoes will keep for 2-4 months
— Most modern homes have basements which are not suitable for storing potatoes but, if you must, make sure you store only sound potatoes, reasonably free from dirt, keeping them away from radiators and hot pipes

Peeling Potatoes

— Hold the potato in one hand and, while rotating it, remove the peel with a vegetable peeler, also cutting out the eyes (good spot for germs to nestle).
— When doing many potatoes, I use a paring knife and peel around the potatoes. The decision to "peel or not to peel" depends on the recipe, but you can decide for yourself. In Europe, potatoes are sold in outdoor markets all peeled and stored in buckets of water. What a convenience for working women and chefs in general!

2

PEI enjoys the reputation as Canada's leading potato province. Producers are always making improvements and enhancing PEI's potato status by anticipating and meeting changing demands in the world market

Farm Gate potatoes have four new potato varieties in 1999: AC Blue Pride, a blue potato; McIntyre, a red potato; Ruby Red, a red potato; and a blight-resistant potato developed on PEI, called Island Sunshine. Some of the English varieties are: Carlingford, Saxon, Rocket and Sierra. Their standard varieties bear such names as Irish Cobbler, Fontenot, Atlantic and Russet Burbank. Prince Edward Island houses a POTATO MUSEUM in a little potato growing village called O'Leary.

BC produces potatoes (spuds) high in iron. The "spud", by the way, gets its name from a special harvesting spade used to dig potatoes in the Andes. I found one on my property when I arrived in Little Fort, BC and took it as a positive portent to grow potatoes. I have since broken the handle and not replaced it, but harvesting potatoes with my bare hands has become one of my greatest pleasures. Finding all those different coloured treasures beneath the earth is an absolute delight and I don't allow anyone to help me dig them up.

Potato Juice

Potato juice has proved very beneficial in healing various ailments. This cleansing is due to the high content of potassium, sulphur, and chlorine in the potato.

Potato juice is beneficial in cleansing the system of toxins, particularly in combination with carrots, in clearing up skin blemishes, and for emphysema. Potato juice along with carrot and celery is a healer for gastric, nerve and muscle disturbances, for gout and sciatica. In such conditions, along with carrot, beet and cucumber juice, people have obtained complete relief from these discomforts in a surprisingly short time, provided they abstained from meat, fowl and fish (Dr. N Walker).

I understand that some folks eat raw potatoes. You can grate them in salads and, combined with a sea vegetable such as arame and a nice garlic miso dressing, quite enjoy them! A new recipe is born.

Starting on page 4 are the "new recipes" you have been waiting for; a little taste of potatoes from around the world.

One never knows when a new and startling use will be found for the incredible potato: Gangster John Dillinger, it is reported, found one when he carved a pistol from a potato, dyed it with iodine, and thus escaped from prison.

Caribbean Lobster Potato Salad

Overall Timing: 30 minutes   *Serves 6-8*

¼ cup	*brown rice vinegar or white wine vinegar*	50 mL
¼ cup	*organic olive oil*	50 mL
8	*green onions, trimmed, thinly sliced*	8
1 tbsp.	*Celtic sea salt*	15 mL
2 tsp.	*crushed chilies*	10 mL
4	*red potatoes, cooked with skins on*	4
2 cups	*fresh corn kernels*	500 mL
1	*red pepper, roasted, peeled, diced*	1
1 lb.	*lobster meat, cooked, cut in 1" (2.5 cm) slices*	500 g

Whisk together the vinegar, oil, green onions, salt, chilies to make dressing. Set aside. Boil potatoes in salted water just until done, about 12 minutes. Remove with a slotted spoon and rinse with cold water, drain, cool, peel, slice thinly and toss with half the dressing. Cook corn until tender and rinse with cold water. Add corn and roasted red pepper to potatoes and toss well. Divide and spoon potato mixture into 4 shallow bowls; top with lobster meat. Drizzle with remaining dressing and serve.

In the 16th century the Inca empire extended for 2,600 miles throughout western South America. They honoured potato spirits by fashioning pottery that blended potato and human forms, thus paying homage to the potato that, along with fish and maize, sustained them and helped them create a great nation.

Incan Potato Arame Salad

Overall timing 20 minutes   *Serves 4*

3	*large, raw, organic potatoes, grated*	3
½	*Spanish onion, chopped*	½
1 cup	*chopped radishes*	250 mL
½-1 cup	*arame seaweed, soaked 15 minutes*	200 mL
½ cup	*chopped green onion*	125 mL

Miso Dressing:

1 cup	*Shiro miso (white miso)*	200 g
½ cup	*rice vinegar*	125 mL
4-6	*garlic cloves, crushed*	4-6

Mix vegetables, drain and rinse seaweed and add dressing. Serve with brown rice or fish.

Greek Potatoes and Feta

Overall timing: 1 hour *Serves 4-6*

1⅓ lb.	*frozen spinach, thawed (2 pkg.)*	600 g
4	*baking potatoes, peeled, cooked, mashed*	4
1	*medium onion, finely chopped*	1
1½ cups	*soft tofu, mashed or equivalent sour cream*	375 mL
2-3 tbsp.	*rice milk (if using tofu) or cream*	25-45 mL
3-4	*garlic cloves, mashed*	3-4
7 oz.	*goat Feta cheese (without rennet), crumbled*	200 g
2 tbsp.	*minced fresh oregano or thyme*	30 mL
1	*lemon, grated peel and juice*	1
2 tsp.	*fine Celtic sea salt*	10 mL
½ cup	*black Greek olives, chopped*	125mL
2 tbsp.	*sesame seeds*	30 mL

Preheat oven to 350°F (180°C). Lightly grease a shallow 9" x 12" (23 x 30 cm) baker. Drain and squeeze liquid from spinach, set aside. Mix onion, tofu, rice milk, garlic, feta cheese, oregano, lemon juice and salt. Spread mashed potatoes in bottom of baker then add a layer of spinach, topping with the tofu feta mixture. Sprinkle with olives and sesame seeds, perhaps some Parmesan cheese. Bake 45 minutes, until bubbly and browned. Serve with a flower salad, Miso soup and sourdough bread.

When traveling from Cairo, Egypt to Aswan near the Sudanese border, to my right I saw nothing but dust, concrete, the odd donkey and a few happy children. To the left all was lush and green. I saw farmers dressed in gilabeas, crouch, tending to their potato gardens. This combination of potatoes and beans was served to me on the train. A beautiful dish, it can be served with a rice pilaf and pita bread.

Egyptian Stew (Khodra Makhluta)

Overall timing 50 minutes. *Serves 6-8*

2 cups	*kidney beans, cooked*	500 mL
4 tbsp.	*organic olive oil*	60 mL
6	*garlic cloves, crushed*	6
1 cup	*chopped onion*	250 mL
3 tsp.	*Celtic sea salt*	15 mL

Egyptian Stew (cont'd)

5	large potatoes, thinly sliced	5
1 tsp.	each cumin and cinnamon	5 mL
½ tsp.	crushed chili peppers	3 mL
3 tbsp.	fresh lemon juice and zest	45 mL
1	large carrot, thinly sliced	1
1 cup	cauliflower florets	250 mL
2 tsp.	honey	10 mL
1½ cups	vegetable broth	375 mL
½ cup	green onion or cilantro, chopped	125 mL

Soak beans overnight; cook 45 minutes or until well done. Place oil, garlic, onions and salt in a large skillet. Sauté over medium heat until onions are translucent. Add potatoes, spices, lemon juice and zest. Cover and steam for 10 minutes, stirring occasionally. Add remaining ingredients, except beans and green onion. Cover and cook for 30 minutes. Add beans and onion, stir, cover and simmer another 10 minutes. Serve with brown rice and pita bread.

In Spain, farmers produce large crops of potatoes. Top the potatoes with aromatic, flavourful olive oil and spices for a taste sensation. Potatoes and other foods were brought from Peru to Spain by the Conquistadors in the 1530s. Nowadays, throughout Spain, tapas dishes such as this are served in Tapas bars.

Potato Tortillas Tapas – Spain

Overall timing 45 minutes   *Serves 4-6*

4	large, waxy potatoes, thinly sliced	4
¼ cup	organic olive oil	75 mL
4	organic eggs	4
2 tsp.	mint or nutmeg	10 mL
½ cup	fresh, finely chopped cilantro	125 mL
2 tsp.	crushed chilies	10 mL
12	flour tortillas–make your own or purchase	12
2-4 cups	spicy lentil salad, page 62	2-4 cups
	slices of Cheddar or tofu cheese	

In a frying pan add oil to a depth of ¼" (1 cm). Heat oil and fry potato slices, a few at a time until soft but not brown. Drain. Beat eggs; add mint, cilantro and chilies, add potato slices, mixing to coat. Heat a small amount of olive oil in a heavy frying pan and add a quarter of the potato mixture, the shape should resemble a pancake. Fry on medium heat until golden brown; flip and fry the other side, then fry remaining potato egg mixture. Warm tortillas in oven. Cut potato mixture in thirds and place in tortillas; add lentil salad, top with cheese, sprinkle with salt, fold to close. Keep warm.

In Bangkok, Thailand, I encountered "floating markets", where farmers and middlemen gather to sell their produce on boats. Pungent smells fill ones' nostrils as flowers and flotillas of food "long boats" float by. Children dive into murky waters and high-speed fish tail boats whiz by. Beside the coconut huskers and live fish sellers are the vegetable boats with pillows of cilantro, green onions, lemon grass, stacks of chilies, hot peppers, red onions, ginger, bean sprouts; mushrooms, garlic and POTATOES.

Asian Potatoes And Prawns

Overall timing: 40 minutes   *Serves 4*

12 oz.	*black tiger prawns, raw, frozen*	*340 g*
½ cup	*spicy Thai cooking sauce*	*125 mL*
1 tsp.	*kudzu or potato starch*	*5 mL*
½ cup	*vegetable broth*	*125 mL*
2 tsp.	*toasted sesame oil*	*10 mL*
3 cups	*matchstick cut waxy potatoes*	*750 mL*
1	*carrot, cut into matchsticks*	*1*
1	*medium onion, chopped*	*1*
3 cups	*chopped bok choi greens*	*750 mL*
1 cup	*shelled peanuts*	*250 mL*
1 cup	*cilantro*	*250 mL*

Place frozen prawns in a medium bowl, cover with cooking sauce, marinate 30 minutes. In another bowl mix kudzu with vegetable broth, set aside. Heat oil in wok or skillet and stir-fry potatoes, carrots, onions and bok choi greens for 5 minutes. Add peanuts, then prawns with marinade sauce, stir-fry for about 2 minutes, until prawns turn pink. Add vegetable broth as needed to thicken, cook for 2 minutes after adding. Taste for seasoning. Serve over rice or kamut pasta. Garnish with cilantro.

Thailand's potatoes are grown in the northern region near Chang Mai. When I travelled there I experienced Chang Mai's Flower Festival; a festival of colourful parades and floats accompanied by good food and music. I enjoyed potato curries throughout Asia and potatoes cooked with lentils or fish. These recipes are already in the book. They are rich and spicy and mouth wateringly delicious.

BC produces fantastic potatoes (I may be slightly prejudiced) especially in the rich alluvial soils of the Lower Mainland, Richmond and the Fraser Valley, Vancouver Island and the Okanagan-Kootenay region. BC grows more potatoes than any other vegetable. Here, near Little Fort—North Thompson-Caribou Region—my garden grows large flavorous heritage potatoes in ancient peat bog soil, a soil filed with chunks of marl and tiny seashells. I add to that lots of local sheep manure and voila. I can harvest potatoes in late July, that's if the neighbors' cows don't get at 'em first! Little Fort is open range country and the cows can clean up the potato patch real quick while waiting to be led down the hill to home. Little Fort's Herefords are prize winners. Could we attribute their sexual prowess and potency to the amount of potatoes they eat?

A savoury pie, served as a main course.

Pumpkin and Potato Pie

Overall timing: 1.5 hours   *Serves 8-10*

Oatmeal Crust:

4 cups	quick rolled oats	1 L
4 cups	spelt wheat flour	1 L
1 cup	sesame oil-organic	250 mL
1 cup	butter	250 mL
2 tsp.	curry powder	20 mL
4 cups	warm, mashed potatoes	1 L
4 cups	cooked, mashed pumpkin	1 L
4 tsp.	Celtic sea salt	20 mL
6 eggs	beaten	6
1 cup	milk or soy milk	250 mL
6	garlic cloves, crushed	6
2	large onions, chopped	2
2-3 tsp.	cumin	10-15 mL

Combine all crust ingredients. Pat into 8" x 10" (20 cm x 25 cm) pan. You may reserve some crust mixture for topping. Boil potatoes in their skins, peel and mash. Mix mashed potatoes and pumpkin with sea salt, eggs, milk. Sauté garlic and onions; add cumin. Add to mashed potato and pumpkin mixture. Pour into crust and bake at 350°F (175°C) for a good hour. Serve with salad and or a light German Potato Butter Soup, page 122. (Can be made ahead and frozen.)

Irish Colcannon Lore

As I stated on page 47, colcannon is traditionally eaten in Ireland on Hallowe'en and various items are placed in the colcannon.

For a dish that is not widely eaten or served today, colcannon remains remarkably well known. Maybe the songs about colcannon are better known than the dish. If you say "Colcannon" in a crowded room in Ireland the chances are that half of the room will break into one version of the song and the other into a completely different version. Like the recipe itself there are two versions commonly known.

Did you ever eat colcannon
when 'twas made with yellow cream
and the kale and praties blended
Like the picture in a dream?
OR:
Did you ever eat and eat, afraid
You'd let the ring go past,
And some old married sprissman
Would get it at the last?

God be with the happy times
When trouble we had not
And our mothers made colcannon
In the little three-legged pot.

Colcannon is so like "champ, cally, stampy and poundies" that it's difficult to understand how it ever came to have so many different names. Yet all over Ireland, colcannon is colcannon and known as nothing else. Although this Irish recipe, see page 47, doesn't conform to my current eating philosophy, it sounded like such fun that I couldn't resist publishing it.

Potatoes With Bangers In Rum Sauce

Overall timing: 2 hours 30 minutes   *Serves: 6-8*

1 lb.	***Shannon traditional sausages (bangers)***	*454 g*
1 cup	***rum (white or dark)***	*250 mL*
6 tbsp.	***dark brown sugar***	*90 mL*
6	***Irish potatoes***	*6*
	herbs—thyme & nutmeg OR rosemary & ginger	

In a skillet with a little oil, cook sausage until lightly browned. Drain on paper towel. Slice sausage into 3 equal parts. Steep in rum for 2 hours; sprinkle with brown sugar, making sure they are covered with liquid. Bake at 325°F (165°C) for 15-20 minutes, or until bubbling. Cook potatoes in their skins in salted water until tender but not overdone. Drain, cool, peel, dice and toss with sea salt and herbs. Cover and keep warm. Serve sausages with cocktail sticks alongside potatoes.

While travelling in exotic Nepal I also feasted on local delicacies of Tibetan and Indian origin. In Kathmandu, in the Thamel district (the heart of the city), I often ate at the Las Kus in the Kathmandu Guest House. Dining in the courtyard garden amongst statues of the Buddha was a much needed tranquil retreat in-between forays into the city and other parts of Nepal.

Hot Potatoes Nepal (Aaloo Wala)

Overall timing: 20 minutes   *Serves: 6-8*

4 cups	*yellow potatoes, cooked in skins, peeled*	*1 L*
¼ cup	*chopped scallions*	*60 mL*
2 tsp.	*Celtic sea salt*	*10 mL*
2 tsp.	*chili powder*	*10 mL*
2 tsp.	*hot pepper sauce or to taste*	*10 mL*
2 tsp.	*cumin*	*10 mL*
2 tsp.	*coriander powder*	*10 mL*
½ cup	*olive oil*	*125 mL*
1-2 tbsp.	*hot mustard*	*8 mL*

Dice potatoes and place in a bowl, add scallions, salt and spices. Mix olive oil with mustard and pour over potatoes. Nice served warm, but may also be served cold. Traditionally served with *Dali Bat*, a rice, lentil and spicy chutney dish.

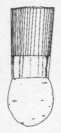

Tibetan Momos: Aaloo Wala is appropriate for "Momos", a Tibetan dumpling that I encountered in the Tibetan sectors of Pokara. There, where local exiled Tibetans live in tiny shanties, and local cafes are not much better than huts, much good comfort food is available. I especially enjoyed sitting with the old women while they were sewing or cooking for festivals. Potatoes are boiled in their skins in gigantic pots and then peeled by the youngsters. After that the young women begin rolling the dough from which the dumpling is made, usually out of white flour, salt and water. Some like to add a bit of yeast or baking soda to the flour water mixture and this gives the wrappers a "doughy" taste. Most of the Tibetans I encountered preferred more filling and less wrapper. You can make a meat filling with ground beef or pork, adding onion, leeks, garlic and a little cilantro. Many hundreds of Momos are made at a time, so when you decide to make them gather your friends and put them to work. When the filling is wrapped in squares of dough, the Momo is steamed and then fried very much like a pirogi.

Bon Appetite!

FRENCH FRIES, APPETIZERS, AND SNACKS

A Word About Deep-Fat Frying

The term means to cook food in enough fat to cover the food completely. When foods are properly deep-fried, a thin coating forms on its outer surface, keeping the juices inside, and preventing the fat from penetrating the food.

Deep-frying is a delicious, ancient way of preparing food. Ancient Romans cooked much of their food in hot olive oil and their descendants in modern Italy still do. The Chinese as well as the French employ deep-frying in their cooking.

Properly prepared deep-fried foods are crisp on the outside but moist and delicate on the inside. They should have absorbed less fat than foods cooked in a lesser amount of fat in a skillet. However, fat absorbtion increases with the length of frying time and the size of the surface exposed to the fat. Therefore, foods to be deep-fried should either take a short time to cook or be precooked. Foods should be no larger than 2-3" (5-7 cm) in diameter and pieces should be uniform in size, to ensure even cooking.

Success with deep-fried foods also depends on the heat of the fat. It must be hot enough to cause quick browning on the food's surfaces, but should not be so hot that it smokes! 375°F (190°C) is an average temperature for deep-frying. All the deep-frying recipes in this book will specify the correct temperature. If you do not use a deep-fryer which automatically sets temperature, you will need a frying thermometer, to measure the heat of the fat. (Keep thermometer in hot water before lowering it into hot fat to prevent cracking). Make sure it is dry before inserting it into hot fat.

A wire basket is helpful when frying French-fried potatoes. The fries are placed into the basket and lowered into hot fat. The basket makes it much easier to get the food in and out and it also ensures even browning.

Fats used in deep-frying should have a high smoking point or heat to a high temperature before burning. Oils, such as peanut, corn, sesame, soy, cottonseed, are all suited to deep-frying, as well as solid fats or lard. Butter and margarine have a low smoking point and are not suitable.

After deep-frying, cool fat and strain through several layers of cheesecloth, coffee filters, or paper towel. Fat may be reused but mark it and keep it for use with foods similar to what it was previously used for. Store in a cool spot or refrigerate.

Thomas Jefferson, U.S.A. president, was once chided for serving this European novelty in the White House, sometime in the early 1700's. While today, French Fries with a capital "F" are hardly nouvelle cuisine, they are national fast food fare.

Jack Simplot, the Idaho "Potato King", sells 5 billion pounds of potatoes a year to McDonalds restaurant chain. He grows the famous Burbank Russet variety (now you know the secret-it's in the potatoes of course and that in Latin goes like this "estar en las papas"). Anyway, Jack has a potato farm so big you could not walk across it in a day, thirty thousand acres of cylindrical potatoes, ideal for French Fries! Imagine a million dollar business rooted in potatoes!

I have included three recipes for French Fries, one is twice fried for extra crispness. I highly recommend frying them twice, they just taste so much better! For maximum flavor and crispness use Idaho, Burbank Russets, or Netted Gems when making French Fries, whenever you indulge of course, which should be now and then. The third method is an oven baking method. It requires very little oil, is low in calories, and is better for you. It should be the method most often used!

Crispy Deep-Fried French Fries

Overall timing: 2 hours, 10 minutes   *Serves: 6*

6-8	**large dry baking potatoes (or enough for the amount of people you are serving)**	6-8
	cold-pressed oil for deep-fryer (or an all-vegetable oil)	
	salt	
	Deep-fryer (a deep-fryer with a basket saves time although a saucepan works fine)	

Scrub potatoes well, peel if desired, then cut potatoes into ¼" (1 cm) slices and chip the potatoes to desired size. Cover with cold water. Let stand in cold water for 2 hours. This releases starch and makes French Fries sweeter. Drain potatoes well and pat thoroughly. This is important or they will spatter when put into hot fat. Heat fat to 375°F (190°C) in deep-fryer and fry potatoes in small batches, 5-8 minutes or until crispy and brown. Fry in small batches because the fat will penetrate the French Fries if they stick together. You may have to stir them to keep from sticking together. Drain a minute in the basket or on paper towels or newspaper. Sprinkle with salt and serve immediately. If you cannot serve immediately, pop into oven and keep warm at 300°F (150°C).

Twice-Fried French Fries

Prepare potatoes as for Crispy French Fries, fry only until light brown, the first time. Drain on paper towels, turn deep-fryer to 400°F (200°C). When fat is very hot, fry French Fries again, a few at a time until golden and crisp. It will take only a few minutes. Drain on paper, sprinkle with salt and serve in a basket. I like to line my basket with a cloth napkin, it looks nice and absorbs oil. Delicious! Mmmmmmmmmm........!

My children grew up on these "ungreasy French Fries". Cooking for me, in those days, was influenced by such books as "Recipes for Healthier Children", by Edith Redman. Good nutrition and healthy foods were number one for most of us in the 70's. Edith Redman's book had many ideas for good nutrition and common sense eating. I use cold-pressed oils, which are much healthier than hydrogenated oils (they have not been heated and have no additives). They store well in the refrigerator and do not acquire a rancid taste.

Instead of the ever popular method of making French Fries, try this for a change. It is quick, and saves calories.

Crispy Low-Cal Oven French Fries

Overall timing: 25 minutes   *Serves: 6*

6-8	medium baking potatoes	6-8
3 tbsp.	cold-pressed oil, peanut is best (or an all-vegetable oil)	45 mL
	salt	

Peel and chip potatoes, (peeling is optional), try them both ways. Arrange chips on 2 cookie sheets, sprinkle oil all over, then salt lightly. Agitate with a fork, making sure all chips are oiled. Put into a preheated oven and bake at 450°F (230°C) for 15 minutes turning once. Finish under the grill, on broil, for a few minutes to brown. Serve immediately in a cloth-lined basket.

Whenever I have made an attempt to grow potatoes, I seemed to have a lot of walnut-sized ones. I have now discovered that it was the lack of water, when tubers began to form, that caused improper development of my potato tubers.

Some people have been known to steal a few little guys from around the plant (to be delicately boiled and served with butter, probably!) In any case, I have included another recipe for those tempting little morsels, which turned out ever so sweet and tasty when I deep-fried them. Look for boiled "new" potato recipes in the dinner and side dish section.

French-Fried Potato Balls

Overall timing: 5 hours, 30 minutes   *Serves: 4-6*

25-30	*fresh new walnut-size boiling potatoes*	*25-30*
	salt	
	water	
	oil, for deep-frying	

Make a salt-water solution of 2 tbsp. (25 mL) salt to 1 quart (1 L) of water. Scrub new potatoes well, put into salt-water for 5 hours or so, this makes the starch turn to sugar and they taste better. Pat potatoes dry, and fry in hot fat 375°F (190°C) a few at a time, until golden, as for French Fries. Drain and refry them for extra good flavor, following directions for Twice-Fried French Fries. Serve immediately with any main course or as an appetizer.

Peruvian natives, were the first to use potatoes for food, along with other roots and peppers. As I stated earlier, the depredation of animals, led to Peruvian vegetarianism. Although there was an abundance of fish in the coastal waters and inland at Lake Titicaca, it was maize (corn) and potatoes which made up the bulk of their diet. Peruvian farmers, over millenia, cultivated the wild potato, growing it high in the mountains where maize would not grow.

New York State is where the potato chip is alleged to have been invented. In 1853, a short-order cook, named George Crum, an American Indian, plotted revenge on a customer who complained about Crum's thick-fried potatoes. In defiance he prepared some superthin slices of potato, deep-fried them, and the rest is history.

Today potato chips are an industry yielding 3 billion dollars a year in the U.S.A., with Canada not far behind.

Potato Chips

Overall timing: 30 minutes   *Serves: 4-6*

4	*large waxy-type or all-purpose potatoes*	*4*
	cold pressed vegetable oil or all	
	vegetable oil	
	salt or seasonings	

Wash or scrub potatoes. No need to peel unless potatoes are old, and the skin is tough. Slice potato paper-thin or pare thin with a vegetable parer or use a kitchen machine with proper slicing blade. Soak sliced potatoes in cold water 15 minutes, then drain and pat dry. Heat oil to 375°F (190°C) in deep fryer or large saucepan, and fry a good handful of potato chips at a time, carefully lowering basket into hot fat. Gently stir chips around in basket, so they do not stick together, and fry quickly, until crisp and splendid. Drain on newspaper or paper towels and salt to taste. Store in a closed jar, after letting chips dry out on newspaper for a few hours.

You may also season with: seasoned salt, garlic salt, celery salt, Italian herbs, dried dill weed and salt, onion salt.

The Spanish conquistadors were the first to merchandise potatoes. When they arrived in Peru, in the early 16th Century, the natives had already developed a method to preserve potatoes, by combining a freezing, drying method. The conquistadors soon became aware of the virtuous potato, fresh or in chunu form, as a food for the masses!

A word about appetizers. Appetizers are hot or cold food, in small portions, and generally served before a meal or as the first course of a meal. The term includes canapés, cocktails, dips, nibblers, hors d'oeuvres, relishes, all of which overlap and are interchangeable.

Canapé — Is a French word, meaning "a couch". In cooking, canapés are small, hot or cold appetizers served on bread, crackers, or a pastry base, so they can be picked up with the fingers. They must be prepared just before serving, so they are crisp and fresh. Delicate foods, such as crab, are best served on plain bread or crackers, whereas, tangy cheese is best on dark bread. Allow 4-6 canapes for each person at a cocktail party where they are served as an appetizer and there is a meal following, more when the cocktail party is the meal.

Hors d'oeuvres — Is a French word meaning, "outside the work". Hors d'oeuvres are hot or cold appetizers, that, unlike canapés, do not have bread or crackers as a base for other foods. Hors d'oeuvres may be eaten with fingers or, at the table, with knife and fork. An immense variety of foods are suited for hors d'oeuvres, but make sure the selections may be served in small portions. Included in this category are vegetables dishes, salads, dressed eggs, fish, meats, chicken livers, pâtés.

Cocktails — Are appetizers that are served at the table with a sauce or dressing and are not to be confused with the alcoholic or nonalcoholic kinds. Along with seafood, fruit and vegetables are most commonly used. Cocktails differ from other types of appetizers, as they are generally served well chilled.

Dips — Are often cold and usually served with vegetables, potato chips, taco chips, crackers, cooked shrimp, frankfurters, or meatballs.

Nibblers — This expression is often used to describe appetizers that can be picked up with the fingers, or with a cocktail pick (small plastic pick, sometimes decorative), or a toothpick. Almonds, peanuts, other nuts,bits of cheese, or pineapple, radishes, carrot sticks or pieces of sweet pepper are often referred to in this way.

Relishes — Relishes include cold crisp vegetables and preserves. In the past relishes were more popular than they are now, especially with farm families. There wasn't a table set until there was a score of homemade relishes on the table. Pickled cucumbers (dills), pickled beets, pickled carrots, pickled watermelon, pickled whatever-there-was-in-abundance. Relishes are still a pride of Mennonite and Pennsylvania Dutch cooking.

Cocktail parties are a popular way of entertaining again. Exotic culinary specialities and finger foods of bite-sized delectables are appearing on the buffet table.

Appetizers should be attractive in shape, color, and garnish and should have interesting flavor and texture combinations.

In the past, appetizers were meant not to fill but to stimulate for the meal to come. Nowadays they are taking on a new role!

What I like about entertaining cocktail party style, is the opportunity to be creative and provide "pretty" food. What I like about cocktail parties mine, or otherwise, is the gastronomic experience, so many delectables in bite-sized proportions.

Craving chocolate, I created this recipe during a midnight cooking spree. Minus the seasonings, plus the chocolate bits and cocoa, this recipe turned out the tastiest chock-full-of-chocolate fritters, that have ever delighted my palate. Judging by the way they disappeared the next morning at breakfast (after a quick warm in the microwave), I would say that the fritters were indeed a success. Serve them hot, for dessert at your cocktail party. (see recipe page 156).

These crisp, seasoned "Petite Potato Puffs", are also tempting on the buffet table, and they freeze well.

Hot Petite Potato Puffs Hors D'Oeuvres

Overall timing: 35 minutes   Makes: about 50 fritters

2½ cups	**cold, mashed potatoes (may be seasoned leftovers), approx. 4 large all-purpose potatoes**	625 mL
1 tsp.	**baking powder**	5 mL
1	**egg**	1
½ cup	**flour**	125 mL
1 tsp.	**chili powder**	5 mL
1 tsp.	**salt**	5 mL
⅛ tsp.	**pepper**	0.5 mL
¼ cup	**milk**	50 mL
1 tsp.	**onion juice**	5 mL
⅛ tsp.	**sherry peppers sauce (optional)**	0.5 mL

Beat together all ingredients until thick and fluffy. Preheat oil to 375°F and drop potato batter, about a rounded teaspoonful at a time into hot fat, fry a few minutes, until brown. Fat should be hot enough so that the puffs brown quickly. Drain on paper towels and serve hot with chili sauce.

To make ahead: Cool fritters before placing in freezer. To reheat simply place on a cookie sheet, heating for 20-30 minutes at 400°F (200°C) or reheat in the microwave for 12-15 minutes.

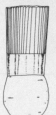

Cocktails are appetizers that are served at the table with a sauce or dressing and they are not to be confused with alcoholic or non-alcoholic beverages. Along with seafood and fruit, vegetables are most commonly used. Cocktails are generally served well chilled

Potatoes Mayonnaise

Overall timing: 3 hours   Serves: 6

4	**medium boiling all-purpose potatoes**	4
3 tbsp.	**dairy sour cream**	4 mL
½ cup	**mayonnaise**	125 mL
⅛ tsp.	**curry**	0.5 mL
	salt and pepper to taste	
1 tbsp.	**freshly chopped parsley**	15 mL

Boil potatoes in their jackets, do not overcook, as they must not be mushy. Cool potatoes, peel, and cut into small cubes. Mix remaining ingredients, and carefully coat cubes with mixture. Chill for 2 hours or more (overnight is fine), serve with toothpicks, at a cocktail party, or in a lettuce-lined sherbet glass before a sit-down dinner.

Potato Cornucopias

Overall timing: 40 minutes   Makes: 2 dozen cornucopias

4	**medium, boiling potatoes**	4
1	**leek or cooking onion**	1
2 tsp.	**chicken soup base**	10 mL
2	**hard-boiled eggs, chopped**	2
½ cup	**cream**	125 mL
24	**slices of ham, salami, or balogna**	24
	lettuce or watercress, garnish	125 mL

Pare and cut potatoes, chop leek into 1" (2.5 cm) pieces, and cook the 2 together in a small amount of water for about 20 minutes, or until tender. Drain and blend or beat on high for a minute, with chicken soup base, chopped egg, and cream. Blend well. Prepare 2 or more platters with a bed of lettuce or watercress. Fill slices of meat with about 1 tbsp. (15 mL) of potato filling and roll into cornucopias. A cornucopia looks like a funnel, being closed at 1 end and open at the other. Fasten meat with a toothpick and place on the bed of greens, toothpick side down. Arrange in a circular manner. Chill. May be made 24 hours before party!

19

Party Potato Turnovers

Overall timing: 1 hour 30 minutes   Makes: 2 dozen

Pastry:

2 cups	flour	500 mL
½ tsp.	salt	2 mL
½ cup	soft butter	125 mL
2	eggs (1 separated)	2
½ cup	sour cream	125 mL

Filling:

1½ cups	cold mashed potatoes (may be leftovers)	375 mL
½ tsp.	salt	2 mL
1 tbsp.	chopped onion	15 mL
1 tsp.	freshly chopped parsley	15 mL
1 tsp.	chicken soup base	5 mL
1 tbsp.	grated Parmesan cheese	15 mL
1	egg	1
1 cup	shredded mozzarella cheese	250 mL

For pastry, cut batter into flour and salt mixture. Stir in 1 egg and the sour cream. Press together into a ball and chill for 1 hour. Meanwhile, beat together the filling ingredients, stir in mozzarella cheese. Roll dough to ⅛" (3 mm) thick. Cut circles, using a wide mouth jar ring or any ring approximately 3" (7 cm) in diameter. Place a generous teaspoonful (5 mL) of potato filling in the center of each circle and fold in half. Press down the edge of pastry with the tines of a fork and place on a cookie sheet to bake.

Beat the extra egg white slightly and brush on the turnovers before baking. Bake at 350°F (180°C) for 30 minutes. The turnovers may be served hot or cold and they freeze well.

In the fall of 1612, the ship "Elizabeth" first brought planting potatoes to Bermuda, from England. Governor Richard Morre arriving in July of the next year, had found a handful of survivors there already with an acre of corn, pumpkins, beans, and wheat. From his journal, "These potatoes flourished exceedingly for a time, till by negligence they were almost lost (all but 2 castaway roots) that have so wonderfully increased, that they are now a maine releef to all the inhabitants." It is interesting to note that the first potatoes cultivated in America came from Bermuda.

Potato Anchovy Fretelse is something different, it sounds suspiciously German, but it hails from Bermuda. A good snack to accompany beer on a warm summer night.

Potato Anchovy Fretelse

Overall timing: 1 hour   Serves: 4

4	**large baking potatoes, well-scrubbed**	4
1-2 tbsp.	**butter**	15-25 mL
1-2	**onions, medium, sliced, in rings**	1-2
15-20	**anchovy fillets, 2 oz. (50 g) can, finely chopped**	15-20
½ cup	**fine bread crumbs**	125 mL
1 tbsp.	**fresh chopped parsley**	15 mL
1 cup	**heavy cream, scalded**	250 mL
½ cup	**grated Parmesan cheese**	125 mL

Cut potatoes as for French Fries. Generously butter a large flat oven-proof casserole. Put in 1 layer of potatoes, another of onions, another of anchovy fillets, small dabs of butter. Top with bread crumbs and parsley and brown at 400°F (200°C) for 15 minutes. Remove from oven, pour hot cream over all, sprinkle with Parmesan cheese; and put back in oven. Bake about 45 minutes at 350°F (180°C). Serve immediately on small plates.

Did you know that eggplant, tobacco and tomatoes are all related to Potåtoes?

In 1621, 20,000 pounds (10,000 kg) of potatoes were exported to the U.S.A., to the state of Virginia, from Bermuda. Only 9 years earlier the stock had been reduced to 2 roots! Within a few years potatoes, along with oranges, became Bermuda's principal exports!

Over in Switzerland, potatoes had flourished as well and were eaten in great quantity. But, when a scourge of scrofula spread across the country in the early part of the 1700's, what other than the misunderstood potato got the blame! The Swiss have since recovered, and developed the potato into a national dish. The following recipe is perhaps the most unusual.

Swiss Raclette

Overall timing: 35 minutes   *Serves: 4-6*

	potatoes	
1-2 lb.	*Gruyère cheese*	*500 g-1 kg*

Boil enough potatoes for the number of people you are serving. New potatoes are preferable. Melt a 1-2 pound (500 g-1 kg) piece of Swiss Gruyère cheese in a pan on top of the stove, over the coals of a campfire or at the side of a fireplace, gradually melting the outside layer of cheese. As it melts, scrape it, warm, onto plates with potatoes.

Note: A "Raclette" grill can be purchased. It is somewhat like a fondue set, although it has a platter instead of a pot, and little flat servers instead of forks. One places the melting cheese on the server and it is warmed on the heated platter. The hot melted cheese is then slipped onto hot cooked potatoes.

A French girlfriend entertains at ladies' luncheons in this manner. She serves raclette with thinly sliced ham and, of course, some good French buns or bread and wine. The potato reigns here with an epicurean fillip, yet nonetheless, it is an unequaled delight over a campfire in the forest!

Sausage-Stuffed Potatoes

Overall timing: 1 hour, 15 minutes; 12-15 minutes microwaved   *Serves: 4*

4	*medium, baking potatoes*	4
4	*pork sausages*	4
4	*bacon slices*	4

Using a corer, make a lengthwise hole through each well-scrubbed potato. Force a sausage through each hole and place potatoes in a small baking dish, wrapping a slice of bacon around each potato.

Bake at 425°F (220°C) basting 3 or 4 times, for an hour, or until tender. Drain off excess fat and serve immediately. Nice with Parmesan tomatoes, page 34.

Somewhere, sometime, you will be taking the peelings from well scrubbed potatoes OFF!

Back in my childhood, I remember having to peel potatoes as part of my "kitchen patrol" at camp. At least 100 potatoes a day passed through the hands of a dozen or so young girls, who happened to be stuck with that particular duty. I cannot recall what became of those "peelin's", but they likely rotted at the Burnaby dump alongside old typewriters and bedsteads.

Instead of throwing your next batch of potato peelin's in the garbage can, place them into a quart jar or plastic container and cover them with salted water before putting the lid on. Sometime within the next week, you should drain the potato peelin's, pat them day, and try this recipe.

Oven-Fried Potato Peelin's

Overall timing: 35 minutes   Serves: 4

	Peelin's from 4-6 large well-scrubbed baking potatoes	
2 tbsp.	melted butter or margarine	25 mL
1 clove	garlic, minced	1
½ tsp.	salt	2 mL
¼ tsp.	freshly ground pepper	1 mL

Sauce:

½ cup	sour cream	125 mL
1 tbsp.	drained bottled horseradish	15 mL
1 tbsp.	chopped chives	15 mL
1 tsp.	prepared mustard	5 mL

Preheat oven to 425°F (220°C). Arrange potato peelin's on a buttered baking sheet in 1 layer. In a small bowl, combine butter, garlic, salt, and pepper, then drizzle and brush mixture over the potato peelin's. Bake for 15 minutes or until lightly browned. Turn peelin's over and bake another 10 minutes or so to brown.

For sauce, combine ingredients, mix well. Serve alongside hot potato peelin's and get dunking!

About a third of the potato's nutrients lie beneath the skin, in what is known as the cortex. It is the narrow band which is visible as a ring on potato chips.

Potato skins and I became aquainted at "The Keg" restaurant.
Potato skins at "The Keg", were deep-fried topped with melted cheese and crisp bacon, and served with a mountain of sour cream!
Try potato skins my way, baked in the oven, for maximum crispness and to reduce calories. You may utilize leftover baked potatoes for potato skins.

Bacon and Cheese Potato Skins

Overall timing: 1 hour, 20 minutes; 20 minutes microwaved *Serves: 4-6*

3	**large baking potatoes, well scrubbed**	*3*
12	*slices of bacon*	*12*
1 cup	*grated Cheddar cheese*	*250 mL*
1 cup	*sour cream*	*250 mL*

Bake potatoes in their skins. Cut baked potatoes into quarters and carefully scoop out the pulp, being careful not to tear the potato shell. Reserve potato insides for another recipe. Place potato skins on a cookie sheet and set aside.

Fry bacon rashers until almost crisp (they should still have a little more cooking to be done) drain and crumble. Grate Cheddar cheese. Begin topping potato skins with crumbled bacon, cheese, and a few more sprinkles of bacon. Preheat broiler and pop the skins under, approximately 6" (15 cm) from the heat, and broil until cheese melts and they are piping hot, about 5-8 minutes.

Serve immediately with sour cream for dunking.

NOTE: To heat in the microwave, put a few skins in at a time, on a microwave-safe plate, repeating until all of the skins are heated and cheese is melted.

Microwave Potato notes . . .

— 4 large potatoes placed in the oven will cook done in 15-18 minutes but wet potatoes may turn gummy inside.

— 3 large boiling potatoes with ¼ cup (50 mL) water in a covered casserole will be done in 12-15 minutes

— 12 small, new potatoes placed in a covered casserole, with ¼ cup (50 mL) water, will cook in 15-20 minutes.

Make up this nutritious shake-and-bake mixture. Store in the refrigerator until hunger strikes your potato lovers. Slice the potato, press chips into mixture.

Potato Chip Treat

Overall timing: 20 minutes   *Serves: 4-6 as a snack*

4	**medium baking potatoes**	4

Shake and Bake Mix

1 cup	**finely crushed cornflakes**	250 mL
½ cup	**grated Parmesan cheese**	125 mL
2 tsp.	**paprika**	10 mL
1 tsp.	**sea salt**	5 mL

Clean potatoes, leaving skins on, slice crosswise into ⅛" slices. Mix finely crushed cornflakes, cheese, paprika and salt, put into a flat dish. Place potato slices, a few at a time, into dish, press into coating mix, coat both sides. Place chips in 1 layer, on a greased cookie sheet. You may need more than 1 pan. Bake at 450°F (230°C) for 10 minutes. Brown under the broiler, if desired, to finish off. Serve immediately.

Chwan Waro Tzu

Overall timing: 30 minutes   *Makes: 3 dozen*

1 lb.	**minced pork**	500 g
1 cup	**mashed potatoes (may be leftovers)**	250 mL
1	**egg**	1
1 tbsp.	**minced bacon**	15 mL
½ cup	**finely minced onion**	125 mL
½ cup	**minced parsley**	125 mL
⅛ tsp.	**cinnamon**	0.5 mL
1 tbsp.	**chopped fresh ginger**	15 mL
1 tbsp.	**soy sauce**	15 mL
2 tbsp.	**cream**	25 mL
	vegetable oil (for deep fyer)	

Sauté pork until lightly brown, drain off fat, add all other ingredients and shape into tiny walnut-sized dumplings. Heat fat in deep-fryer to 375°F (190°C) and cook dumpling for 2-3 minutes, or until lightly browned. Serve with soy sauce. According to true Chinese fashion, the little dumplings are floated in sauce and eaten with rice.

Quesadillas are of Mexican origin, and are prepared in Mexico with a hand-made shell. We have tried the filling in pita bread, an East Indian pocket bread, as well as in taco shells and green pepper shells.

Shane's Quesadillas

Overall timing: 20 minutes   Serves: 2 ravenous teens

Tacos or Pita bread

Filling:

2 cups	mashed potatoes (may be leftovers)	500 mL
1	onion, chopped	1
1	jalepeño pepper, chopped (optional, they are HOT!)	1
¼	green sweet pepper, chopped	¼
¼ cup	chopped pitted black olives	50 mL
½ tsp.	garlic salt	2 mL
½ tsp.	sherry peppers sauce (optional)	2 mL
1 tsp.	Worcestershire sauce	5 mL
½ cup	gravy or chicken bouillon	125 mL
	chunks of soft cheese	

Mix all ingredients together, adding any other spices or leftovers to taste, and mix with gravy or chicken bouillon. Heat filling in a frying pan for 5 minutes and stuff your favourite shell, topping with chunks of soft cheese such as Monterey Jack or havarti.

Potato Nachos

Lightly spread Quesadillas filling on nacho chips, place on a microwave safe plate. Top with grated Cheddar cheese, instead of a soft cheese, and warm in the microwave until cheese melts and bubbles. Serve immediately.

Exercise is not a drudge. Working out should not be a daily chore, it should become a lifetime habit. Besides the obvious physical benefits, it provides an overall feeling of exhilaration.

BREAKFAST
SUGGESTIONS

Fine Hash Browns with Cracklings to Get You Crackin'

As a young girl, there was nothing more enticing than fresh-baked white bread, smothered in cracklings. (Nowadays of course I eat very little white bread and generally don't smother it in anything!) Anyway, now you may ask, what do cracklings and fresh bread have to do with potato recipes? Well, as a kid I rated potatoes about one notch above grilled liver. Sorry Mom. I had to be cajoled into eating potatoes, by smothering them in cracklings. Canadian Mennonites used to make their own cracklings when pig butchering was still kind of a "bee". Now one has to search for them in delicatessens.

Cracklings are crispy brown pork or goose bits left after rendering solid fats and they are substituted for butter. They are delicious.

Fine Hash Browns

Overall timing: 30 minutes   Serves: 4-6

4-6	dry baking potatoes	4-6
1	onion finely chopped	1
4 tbsp.	cracklings, or 2 tbsp. (25 mL) butter or bacon fat — 8 tbsp. — if you dare	60 mL
	salt and pepper to taste	

For fine hash browns, simply grate washed, peeled potatoes and let rest for 15 minutes. (Time to get your eggs baking.). Then squeeze out excess water and stir-fry in frying pan along with the onion and cracklings. Brown until crisp, about 10 minutes. Just a few minutes before they are done, season and serve alongside your favorite eggs.

Variations:
— Add ½ cup (125 mL) chopped fresh mushrooms 2-3 minutes before hash browns are done.
— Add 2-3 slices chopped bacon in frying pan, reducing fat.
— Add ½ cup (125 mL) ground sausage meat, reduce fat.
— Add 1 tsp. (5 mL) chili powder for the last few minutes.
— Add 2 crushed cloves of garlic in frying pan.
— Add ½ cup (125 mL) chopped green pepper to frying pan.

Heavenly Hash Browns

Overall timing: 25 minutes   Serves: 4

3	*boiling potatoes*	*3*
1	*onion*	*1*
2	*egg whites, lightly beaten*	*2*
½ tsp.	*salt*	*2 mL*
¼ tsp.	*freshly grated pepper*	*1 mL*
⅛ tsp.	*garlic powder*	*0.5 mL*
	fat for frying	

Peel and grate potatoes and onion. Stir in egg whites. Add salt, pepper, and garlic powder. Drop by the tablespoon (15 mL) into ¼" (1 cm) deep fat. Turn and brown other side, a few minutes. Drain on paper towel. Serve hot. Terrific with bacon and eggs.

Did you know that the carbohydrates in potatoes are readily digestible? Canada's Food Guide recommends at least one serving of potatoes a day as they are important sources of many nutrients. One potato supplies about as many calories as a fairly large apple.

Chunky Hash Browns

Overall timing: 30 minutes   Serves: 4-6

4-6	*small boiling potatoes, unpeeled*	*4-6*
2 tbsp.	*butter*	*25 mL*
1 tsp.	*seasoned salt*	*5 mL*
1 tbsp.	*freshly chopped parsley*	*15 mL*
	caraway seeds	
2 tbsp.	*butter for frying*	*25 mL*

Cut potatoes into 1" x ⅛" (5 cm x 3 mm) thick rounds. Boil in a small amount of water for 8 minutes. Melt butter in frying pan, drain potatoes. Sprinkle drained potatoes generously with seasoned salt and freshly chopped parsley. Toss with a little flour. Add caraway seeds if you wish. Stir-fry in butter for 8-10 minutes. Serve hot with scrambled eggs, English muffins, or sautéed apple rings.

NOTE: Make your own seasoned salt, to avoid additives.

Hashed Potatoes with Eggs

Overall timing: 1 hour   Serves: 6

4 cups	*boiling potatoes, peeled, boiled, grated*	*1 L*
2 cups	*cooked, ground lean beef, chicken or turkey*	*500 mL*
1 onion	*chopped*	*1*
	salt and pepper to taste	
2 tsp.	*chili powder*	*10 mL*
6	*small eggs*	*6*

In a very large frying pan, melt a little butter or margarine, add potatoes, meat, onion, salt, pepper and chili powder. Stir all together. Flatten with the back of a spoon. Cook slowly over low heat. Cook about 10 minutes, then turn carefully with a large pancake turner, or a round piece of stiff cardboard, cut to fit under the hash. When you have this masterpiece turned over, make 6 hollows in the hash with the back of a spoon. Drop an egg into each hollow. Cover frying pan and turn heat down to low. Cook slowly until eggs are set to desired doneness.

Now, carefully slide the hash onto a heated platter.

In the early days, this "new potato vegetable" became fashionable in some European circles, although it was mainly boiled or baked. Hashed potatoes were invented much later in America and along with other hashes, became extremely popular.

In the early 1800's, other ingredients were added to potatoes and the gourmet potato arrived. Potatoes were eaten with butter, salt and imported spices, the juice of oranges and lemons, and double refined sugar! In England they were thought to . . . increase seed, and provoke lust, causing fruitfulness in both sexes. But people largely remained unconvinced of the value of the simple tuber which was to become an excellent food for the masses.

English Potato Fritters

Overall timing: 40 minutes   *Serves: 4-6*

4	large, boiling potatoes	4
2	egg yolks, large	2
1 tsp.	salt	5 mL
¼ tsp.	freshly ground pepper	1 mL
1 tbsp.	potato starch (also called potato flour)	15 mL
2	egg whites	2
	butter	

Cook and peel potatoes. Press potatoes through a ricer or mash them. Beat in next 4 ingredients. Beat egg whites until stiff. Fold whites into potato mixture, very gently. Heat butter in a skillet to a depth of ¼" (1 cm). Drop mixture by tablespoonfuls into hot butter, butter should not be so hot that it smokes! Fry until crisp and golden, turning once. Serve with applesauce or sour cream.

Solanum, the potato's genus, includes more than 2000 species and about 160 are tuber bearing. "Solanum Tuberosum" is the common potato known worldwide. Wild potatoes were found as far north as Nebraska, U.S.A., nonetheless no species were cultivated outside South America at the time that the Spanish arrived in the "New World". Until the 1930's, it was believed that the potato originated in the U.S. Geneticist N. I. Vavilov, showed this to have been impossible.

Nebraska Omelet

Overall timing: 30 minutes   *Serves: 3-4*

6	eggs	6
½ tsp.	salt	2 mL
½ tsp.	freshly ground pepper	2 mL
1	onion, in chunks	1
1 tbsp.	freshly chopped parsley	15 mL
3	boiling potatoes, cooked, quartered	3
2 tbsp.	butter	25 mL

Blend eggs in blender for 30 seconds. Add other ingredients, except butter. Coarsely chop. Heat butter in large skillet, add contents of blender. Brown over medium heat, 10 minutes. Pop under broiler to nicely brown top. Great with back bacon and chili sauce.

Australian Shrimp and Potato Cakes

Overall timing: 45 minutes   *Serves: 4-6*

1 lb.	fresh shrimp, chopped	500 g
1 cup	water	250 mL
1 large	onion, chopped	1
1	bay leaf	1
2	cloves	2
2 cups	mashed potatoes (may be leftovers)	500 mL
¼ tsp.	nutmeg	1 mL
½ cup	hot cream	125 mL
2	eggs	2
2 tbsp.	butter	25 mL

Cook the shrimp in water with onion, bay leaf, and cloves, for 2-3 minutes. Stir drained shrimp into mashed potatoes, discarding bay leaf and cloves, add nutmeg, cream and eggs. Mix well. If somewhat soft, you may add 1-2 tbsp. (15-25 mL) flour. Fashion into flat 2" (5 cm) cakes and sauté in butter on both sides until brown and crisp. Serve with cheese-curry biscuits or Parmesan tomatoes (page 34).

Stir-Fried Zucchini Sticks for 6

2	10-12" (25-30 cm) zucchini squash	2
	bread crumbs	
	Parmesan cheese	

Slice zucchini into 2" x ½" (5 cm x 1.3 cm) sticks, unpeeled. Place in frying pan and stir-fry in a little butter for 5 minutes.
Sprinkle with bread crumbs and grated Parmesan cheese.

The potato was banned in Burgundy, France, in 1619, because the people were persuaded that "too frequent use of potatoes caused leprosy". This idea, however untrue, persisted in France well into the eighteenth century. It was not until one ebullient individual, Antoine Viard, decided to publish a potato recipe in his cookbook, "Le Cuisinier Imperial", that the potato was seriously looked at by the French. The potato has since been developed into high art by French cooking masters.

This potato omelet called "Crique À L'Ancienne" is somewhat different from the Nebraska omelet, in that it employs grated raw potato. Chopped dill adds a delicate different flavor.

Crique A L'Ancienne (Potato Omelet)

Overall timing: 30 minutes   Serves: 6

3	medium baking potatoes	3
8	large eggs	8
1 tsp.	salt	5 mL
¼ tsp.	freshly ground pepper	1 mL
¼ cup	milk	50 mL
¼ cup	finely chopped, fresh dill or 2 tsp. (10 mL) dill weed	50 mL
8	drops Tabasco sauce	8
2 tbsp.	butter	25 mL

Pare and finely grate potatoes. Beat eggs just enough to mix whites and yolks. Add salt, pepper, milk, chopped dill, grated potatoes, and Tabasco sauce. Heat butter over moderate heat in a large skillet or omelet pan and pour in egg mixture, it should be about ½" (1.3 cm) thick.

Cover skillet and cook over low heat until eggs are set and potato is cooked, about 20 minutes. Serve hot and pass the Camembert cheese!

The nutrional value of potatoes is now being understood. It never was the poor, nutritious, potato that piled on inches. Men and woman are now eating for inner health, and slimming the thighs to asparagus sticks is a thing of the past.

"Kugel" is the general Hebrew term for casserole. Here is one with the almighty potato. This dish is light and flavorful and resembles a soufflé. I have altered the recipe from the traditional Jewish preparation, as some of the rules of preparation in Jewish recipes are important for religious reasons but not necessary for culinary reasons.

The original recipe calls for matzoth flour which is used in cooking during Passover. White unbleached flour substitutes nicely. Kugel is good with baked Parmesan tomatoes or stir-fried zucchini sticks.

Potato Kugel

Overall timing: 50 minutes   Serves: 6

3	**eggs, separated**	*3*
6 medium	**baking potatoes, peeled, cooked, mashed and kept warm**	*6*
1 tbsp.	**minced onion**	*15 mL*
1 tsp.	**salt**	*5 mL*
½ tsp.	**garlic powder**	*2 mL*
	freshly ground pepper	
5 tbsp.	**unbleached white flour (or same amount of matzoth bread crumbs)**	*75 mL*
¼ cup	**chicken soup broth**	*50 mL*

First beat the egg yolks in a bowl and blend them with the mashed potatoes, onion, salt, garlic powder, pepper, flour, and broth. The well-blended mixture should be firm but not dry. Beat the egg whites until stiff and carefully fold them into the potato mixture, so they remain airy. Preheat the oven to 400°F (200°C). Lightly grease the inside of a 3-4 quart (3-4 L) casserole with butter and bake the kugel for 20-30 minutes. The top should be firm and brown. Serve hot.

Baked Tomato Parmesan for 6

3	**tomatoes**	*3*
	Parmesan cheese	

Halve tomatoes and place on greased baking sheet. Sprinkle with grated Parmesan cheese. Bake for 15 minutes at 400°F (200°C).

"Hanukkah" celebrates the heroism of Mattathias, who defied Antiochus in the 2nd Century B.C. At that time a miracle occurred.

Nowadays, in Jewish homes, candles are lit each night of this religious celebration and there are usually games and gifts for the family. Latkes, or potato pancakes, are traditional. They are not similar in texture to hotcakes or crêpes. They are served with sour cream or puréed fruit (applesauce).

Potato Pancakes or Latkes

Overall timing: 25 minutes   *Serves: 4 (Makes a baker's dozen of 2½-3" (6-7 cm) cakes)*

4	*medium waxy potatoes*	*4*
1 tbsp.	*grated onion*	*15 mL*
1	*large egg*	*1*
⅓ cup	*stoneground whole-wheat flour*	*75 mL*
1 tsp.	*salt*	*5 mL*
½ tsp.	*freshly ground pepper*	*2 mL*
	oil for frying	

Peel and finely grate potatoes. Squeeze out some of the moisture in the grated potato, I find my hands work best for this. Add other ingredients, beat well with a wooden spoon. Put ¼" (1 cm) oil in frying pan and heat. Drop rounded tablespoonfuls (15 mL) of batter into hot fat and flatten with the back of the spoon. Fat should be hot enough that the pancakes brown in about 2-3 minutes. Turn and brown other side, keep warm. Serve with sour cream, puréed fruit, or a mixture of yogurt and chives.

Variations
Herbed Latkes — Here's a perked up recipe for Latkes.
   To basic recipe add:

1 tsp.	*parsley flakes*	*5 mL*
½ tsp.	*crumbled rosemary leaves*	*2 mL*
¼ tsp.	*ground sage*	*1 mL*
⅛ tsp.	*garlic powder*	*0.5 mL*

Scrambled Eggs and Sausage on Potato Latkes —
   Cook a sausage patty for each potato latke, place it on latke, making a well in the center with back of spoon.
   Scramble 6 eggs for 4 people, with parsley and spices, and place a rounded spoonful on top of sausage.

"Blintzes" are also a Jewish tradition. They are rolled, stuffed crêpes, similar to a French crêpe but a little heavier in texture. Generally made with cottage cheese or a fruit filling, these have a vegetarian twist, potato and onion filling.

Potato-Onion Blintzes

Overall timing: 1 hour, 30 minutes   *Serves: 6*

Crêpe:

3	eggs	3
1½ cups	sifted whole-wheat flour	375 mL
1¾ cups	milk	425 mL
½ tsp.	salt	2 mL

Filling:

2 cups	warm mashed potatoes (may be leftovers)	500 mL
1	onion, chopped	1
1	egg, beaten	1
½ tsp.	Italian Herb Seasoning	2 mL
½ tsp.	salt	2 mL
¼ tsp.	freshly ground pepper	1 mL

White Sauce:

1 tbsp.	butter	15 mL
1 tbsp.	flour	15 mL
1 cup	milk	250 mL
½ tsp.	freshly ground pepper	2 mL
¼ tsp.	Italian Herb Seasoning	1 mL
⅛ tsp.	prepared mustard	0.5 mL

In a large mixing bowl, beat crêpe ingredients, until smooth. Let sit for an hour. (Best if refrigerated overnight or 6 hours). Melt a little butter or use oil in a frying pan or crêpe pan, heat until it smokes. Pour a little batter into pan, lift and tilt the pan so the batter covers the bottom. Cook a minute or so, turn and cook the other side. Stack crêpes on a plate and keep warm in the oven.

Beat filling until fluffy, spoon 2 tbsp. (15 mL) on center of crêpe. Roll up, fold ends under, place on greased cookie sheet. Dab with butter, pop under the broiler a few minutes, until lightly browned.

Meanwhile, make white sauce. Melt butter in a saucepan and sprinkle in the flour, stirring rapidly to blend. Slowly add the milk, again stirring constantly to remove all lumps. Place over high heat and bring to a light boil. Add seasonings. Serve alongside blintzes.

Baked Potato Nests with Eggs

6	large baking potatoes, peeled, cooked, mashed	6
2 tbsp.	butter	25 mL
1 tbsp.	freshly chopped parsley	15 mL
1 tsp.	salt	5 mL
¼ tsp.	freshly ground pepper	1 mL
	forcing bag for piping mashed potatoes	
1	egg, beaten, for glaze	1
8	small eggs	8
	sprigs of parsley	

Mash potatoes with butter, parsley, salt, and pepper. Cool a little. Pipe creamy mashed potatoes onto a greased cookie sheet to form 8, 2" (5 cm) nests. Glaze nests with beaten egg, and break 1 small egg into each nest. Bake at 400°F (200°C) for 5 minutes or until eggs are set to your liking. Garnish with parsley and serve plain or with bacon or sausages.

*These potato nests can be used as a nouvelle cuisine on the dinner plate. Simply bake as directed, but without eggs, brown nicely and fill with a mélange of steamed garden vegetables. The vegetables you choose should be finely chopped. Freshly steamed, baby garden peas are simply perfect.

Mr. Thomas Hughes, a modern American potato crusader, takes offense with the potato's social bruising. Mr. Hughes has founded and curates the POTATO MUSEUM, in the village of Lanse-Maransart, Belgium. He strongly feels that the potato is still the world's most misunderstood food and he feels badly that the food which made possible the industrial revolution gets such a bum rap in history reports! Mr. Hughes decided to found the museum to give the potato its historical due. Commendable!

The museum contains exciting potato trivia such as stamps from Tristan da Cuhna, (which cost 4 potatoes each), potato peelers, and diverse documentation. One such documentation is of the "Kartoffelkreig" — potato war, which was fought between the Prussians and the Austrians in 1778-1779.

The war received its name after the clashing armies ate up all the potatoes along the battle lines in Bohemia and then called off all the fighting.

This "Petite Crêpes of Potato" recipe is from a restaurant in Ardennes, Belgium. The regional cooking here is greatly influenced by both German and French cooking. It is an area of rich tilled farmlands, cold rivers, and pine forests. In Belgium, as well as many parts of France, petite potato pancakes often appear served with main course dishes such as stuffed duck legs and freshly caught trout. The potato batter may be made beforehand and refrigerated until cooking time.

Petite Crêpes of Potato (Hostellerie Saint-Roch)

Overall timing: 1 hour   *Serves: 6*

1⅓ cups	**peeled, boiled, and riced baking potatoes, about 1 pound (500 g)**	*325 mL*
3	**medium eggs**	*3*
¾ cup	**whipping cream**	*175 mL*
¼ cup	**unbleached white flour**	*50 mL*
	salt	
1 tsp.	**brown sugar**	*5 mL*
	butter	

In a blender or food processor, blend the potatoes, eggs, cream, flour, salt, and sugar until the batter is smooth. Transfer batter to a bowl and let stand for 30 minutes. Heat a griddle or a heavy skillet to moderate heat, and brush with butter. Stir batter, drop by teaspoon (5 mL) onto the griddle to form 1" (2.5 cm) rounds, and cook the crêpe for 30 seconds or so, until bubbles appear on the surface. Turn crêpe, cook other side until golden. Transfer to a heated platter. You may keep the crêpe warm in the oven at 250°F (120°C). Serve hot!

FOR OVERNIGHT REFRIGERATION

Prepare the batter, refrigerate. Let stand at room temperature for at least 2 hours before heating the grill and beginning to cook crêpes.

Potsosi (Peru) silver mineworkers subsisted almost entirely on a dehydrated form of potato called "chunu". Before too long, speculators were streaming across the Atlantic from Spain to buy supplies from chunu producers in the mountains and resell them at inflated prices to the mineworker slaves, returning home not only considerably richer, but with potato stock as well. By 1573 potatoes were blossoming all over Spain.

"For a hearty breakfast after an early morning ski ...
Put on a pot of rich full-bodied coffee ...
Light the fire ...

Himmel und Erde (Potatoes with Apples)

Overall timing: 40 minutes   Serves: 8

2 tbsp.	brown sugar	25 mL
2 tsp.	salt	10 mL
½ tsp.	freshly ground pepper	2 mL
2 cups	cold water	500 mL
8	medium dry potatoes, scrubbed, cut into 1" (2.5 cm) cubes	8
4	tart cooking apples, cored and quartered (Gravenstein or MacIntosh)	4
1 lb.	lean bacon, diced	500 g
2	medium onions, sliced ½" (1.3 cm) thick, separated into rings	2
1 tsp.	cider vinegar	5 mL

In a heavy skillet combine sugar, 1 tsp. (5 mL) of the salt, pepper and water. Add potatoes, apples and bring to a boil over high heat. Reduce heat to moderate and cover skillet tightly. Simmer undisturbed until the potatoes are tender but not falling apart. Drain.

Meanwhile in a 10" (25 cm) skillet, cook the diced bacon until done but not too crisp. With a slotted spoon, remove bacon to paper towels to drain. Add onion rings to remaining fat, cook over moderate heat for 5-8 minutes, or until rings are soft. Drain off fat, leaving a tbsp. (15 mL) or so with the onions.

Just before serving, stir in the remaining teaspoon (5 mL) of salt and the vinegar into potatoes and apples and taste for seasoning. Transfer the contents to a heated bowl, top with onion rings and diced bacon.

"Gather around for good food and good times!"

Did you know that the average, annual world crop of potatoes — 295 million tons (262 million t) (1984) could cover a four-lane highway and circle the world at least 6 times?

By 1600, groundnuts or peanuts were familiar to the Spaniards. They had encountered them in Haiti. The variety which they found in Peru also soon traveled with them.

However, the potato was entirely new and, when the conquistadors returned, they referred to potato dishes as "a dainty dish even for Spaniards".

Potatoes were introduced into Europe through Spain. From Spain they went to Italy, England, France and Germany.

Dainty Potato Patties Conquistador

Overall timing: 40 minutes   *Serves: 6 (2 servings each)*

2 cups	cold, mashed potatoes (may be leftovers)	500 mL
1	egg, beaten	1
1	onion, minced	1
2 tbsp.	tomato paste	25 mL
1 tsp.	salt	5 mL
1 tsp.	paprika	5 mL
	flour or crushed cereal (unsweetened variety)	

Combine and beat well; mashed potatoes, egg, onion, tomato paste, spices. Shape into 12 dainty patties and roll in flour or cereal. Brown slowly in butter, about 5 minutes on each side. Nice with broiled sausages.

For a quick light supper I add 1 cup (250 mL) of cooked crab or salmon to this recipe. I serve them in hamburger rolls, "à la fish burger!" Don't forget to spread the roll with tartar sauce and slip in the greens.

Did you know that the French employ the pomme de terre at almost every meal? "It enhances the taste and gives a softness to the meal".

There is no denying that the best and most convenient methods for cooking potatoes are boiling and baking (in their own jackets) provided that the potatoes are fresh. The world's best cooks are adamant that the skins should not be gashed before cooking, as any opening in the skin allows moisture to escape and results in a somewhat drier potato.

When last season's potatoes have become soft and starchier, try this Irish recipe. German cookbooks also offer "Hopel Popel", minus the cheese, plus scrambled eggs.

Hopel Popel

Overall timing: 45 minutes   Serves: 4

4	**boiling potatoes, washed, thinly sliced**	4
6	**strips bacon, diced**	6
1	**onion, finely chopped**	1
½ cup	**chopped fresh mushrooms**	125 mL
4	**eggs, large**	4
1 tsp.	**salt**	5 mL
½ tsp.	**freshly ground pepper**	2 mL
½ cup	**grated strong Cheddar cheese**	125 mL
1 tbsp.	**freshly chopped parsley**	15 mL
1 tsp.	**caraway seeds**	5 mL

Cook potatoes in a small amount of water. Meanwhile, in a large frying pan, cook bacon, onion, and mushrooms. Fry until tender. Add drained cooked potatoes to bacon mixture in frying pan, mix well. Heat through. Beat eggs with salt and pepper and pour over mixture. Do not stir. Sprinkle with cheese, parsley, caraway seeds and cook covered, at very low heat until eggs are set. Brown under the broiler, 6" (15 cm) from heat. Cut into wedges to serve.

NOTE: This potato dish is one where the starch content is important. The starchier the potato the better it will stick together and cut into wedges. A quick starch test is to rub together cut potato halves. The white froth which appears is the starch. Stick the cut surfaces together and hold the potato up. The halves of a starchy potato will adhere, whereas, a low starch potato will not hold together at all.

The Irish population exploded, after the potato was introduced. By 1845 it had passed eight million, which is more than double the present population. 10-14 pounds of potatoes were eaten a day, on the average, by an adult.

One benefit of being an Air Force wife, is the occasional trip abroad. If that happens to be somewhere with sun, sea, and good food, all the better. During a reprieve to Bermuda, (which was around the time I began eating, sleeping, and breathing potatoes) I fell in love with the island's unique, often slightly sweet, potatoes and sherry peppers sauce. I purchased a good supply of "Outerbridges' Sherry Peppers Sauce" and a few cookbooks to bring home. O.S.P. Sauce is built with spices and tiny bird peppers and macerated in sherry over a period of time. Experimenting with potatoes, I found that this sauce zests up potato dishes in a wonderful way. I have included it in several recipes. Don't panic! There are similar sauces available in Canada. Experiment! It is exported to the U.S.A., so keep it on your shopping list when traveling south, or to beautiful Bermuda.

Make this pie the day before and serve it cold for a special brunch or breakfast. It is very nice for Christmas breakfast. The French have a pork pie called tourtière, usually made with ground beef and pork. I have made this pie with ground moose meat! As all wives of hunters are aware, moose dishes can be the piéce de résistance of winter cooking. My version is quite simple and I think you will find it simply delicious.

Sherry Peppers Pork Pie

Overall timing: 1 hour, 20 minutes   *Serves: 8-10*

Pastry:

½ tsp.	baking powder	2 mL
2 tsp.	salt	10 mL
2 tbsp.	brown sugar	25 mL
3 cups	unbleached white flour	750 mL
1 cup	lard	250 mL
1	egg, beaten	1
1 tbsp.	white vinegar	15 mL
½ cup	cold water	125 mL

Filling:

2 lbs.	ground pork	1 kg
2 cups	mashed potatoes (may be leftovers)	500 mL
2 tsp.	salt	10 mL
1 tsp.	sherry peppers sauce	5 mL
2	cloves garlic, crushed	2

To make pastry, add the baking powder, salt, and brown sugar to the flour, stir. Cut in the lard, until mixture is well mixed and crumbly. Combine wet ingredients, then stir gently into flour mixture with a fork and press the dough together.

Sherry Peppers Pork Pie (continued)

Divide the dough in half and roll out 2 pieces to fit a deep 10" (25 cm) pie plate. Place the bottom crust in the pie plate. Refrigerate while you prepare the filling.

For filling, sauté the fresh pork in a large pan until soft and pink color disappears. Drain off excess fat, leaving a ¼ cup (50 mL) juices in the pan. Add mashed potatoes, salt, peppers sauce, and crushed garlic. Mix well. Put meat mixture into pie plate.

Into center of top pastry crust, cut a 1" (2.5 cm) steam hole and put in place, pressing down edges firmly. Brush the top with milk and bake at 375°F (190°C) for 45-50 minutes. Serve hot or cold.

Potatoes can be made into alcohol. Researchers in the U.S.A. have shown that one acre of potatoes yields approximately, 1200 gallons (5400 L) of ethyl alcohol in a year. Henry Ford predicted that the world would soon run out of cheap petroleum and decided to make ethyl alcohol, from potatoes, to use as fuel to burn in cars. The "affair" went down like the Edsel, although now-a-days it seems like a better idea!

The potato is a good source of phosphorous, it builds bone, brain and nerves; potassium, necessary for construction of cells in the body; and iron, which removes wastes from the body.

With "Onion and Parsley Sauce" (below), as with any other sauce — do not overcook — as some herbs and flavoring ingredients lose their zest in about 5 minutes!

Ancient Chinese Secret: Be not caught with underseasoned foods or you be not considered good cook.

Potato Cakes with Onion and Parsley Sauce

Overall timing: 25 minutes   Serves: 4-6

Pancakes:

1½ cups	leftover mashed potatoes, cooled	375 mL
3	large eggs	3
3 tbsp.	cream	45 mL
2 tbsp.	unbleached white flour	25 mL
1 tsp.	baking powder	5 mL
½ tsp.	salt	2 mL
½ cup	scalded milk	125 mL

Sauce:

1	onion minced	1
½ cup	minced fresh parsley	125 mL
¾ cup	butter	175 mL

Beat together potatoes, eggs, cream, flour, baking powder, salt. Beat in scalded milk. Cook on a greased griddle, in rounds, about 2" (5 cm) in diameter. Flatten with a fork, turning once. When brown, remove from griddle and keep warm until serving.

For sauce, cook onion and parsley in butter over low heat, 3 minutes, or until onion is soft. Divide pancakes into 6 servings and spoon sauce over pancakes to serve.

LUNCH IDEAS
AND SALADS

Luncheon menus and salads need not be unimaginative. Simple but sumptuous, the dishes which are included here are for the gourmet and the down-to-earth cook. There are old Irish favorites such as Haggerty, which looks like a jumbo pancake, oozing with rich Cheddar cheese; Colcannon, which is a potato and kale dish called "thump" in the Midlands, and "champ" in the north and west. American chicken hash and Potatoes and Hominy Sauté have good honest flavors! For all with a little gourmet in us, Creamed Mushroom and Wine Potatoes and Potato Soufflé are tempting fare.

Robert E. Rhoades, in his worldwide potato pilgrimage, found no people who pay more respect to the potato than the Irish. Per capita, only East Europeans eat more potatoes. An Irish saying goes," Potatoes and marriage are two things too serious to joke about!" How true.

Rich, but delicious . . .

Irish Haggerty

Overall timing: 35 minutes   *Serves: 4*

3	medium, boiling potatoes, paring optional	3
1	large onion	1
1 tbsp.	bacon fat	15 mL
1 cup	grated sharp Cheddar cheese	250 mL
1 tsp.	salt	5 mL
½ tsp.	freshly ground pepper	2 mL

Cut potatoes into paper thin slices, pat dry. Slice onion very thin. Heat bacon fat in a small, heavy frying pan and place alternate layers of potato, onion, cheese, finishing with potatoes. Sprinkle each layer with salt and pepper. Place slabs of bacon fat on top of potatoes until done, approximately 25 minutes. Brown under the broiler. Cut into wedges and serve hot.

Nice with Parmesan tomatoes, see recipe page 34.

At our house, special occasions, any excuse to celebrate, call for special food. Alongside our long-range agendas are spontaneous happenings, which the children and adults enjoy together. For "Andrews' Gourmet Night", we research cookbooks from other nations for unusual recipes and customs. The children choose a country and help to create culinary specialties. Imagination, garnished with a lot of enthusiasm, is a good recipe for fellowship and good times.

Party Colcannon, a delectable mix of buttered kale and potato, originates in Ireland, and is served on Halloween. A ring is stirred into the mixture and foretells the future. Whoever finds the ring shall be the next to be married!

Party Colcannon

Overall timing: 35 minutes   Serves: 6

6	**boiling potatoes, pared**	6
1	**onion, chopped**	1
1 tbsp.	**butter**	15 mL
1 tsp.	**salt**	5 mL
¼ tsp.	**freshly ground pepper**	1 mL
½ cup	**hot cream**	125 mL
1	**small head kale, finely chopped**	1
	butter	

Separately cook potatoes and kale in a small amount of water. Drain. Save the water! Mash potato and mix in onion, butter, salt, pepper, cream and kale. Reheat thoroughly and mound on a plate. (Don't forget to stash a ring in the mixture for fun). Fill the center with a generous dab of butter, give everyone seated around the table a fork and a glass of buttermilk for accompaniments.

A single potato can supply half the daily Vitamin C requirement of an adult (23 mg). An important factor which sea captains surmised about when they took potatoes aboard ship to prevent scurvy among their crews. If they had been castaways on an island for a year, 20 pounds (10 kg) of potatoes, could have grown a ton of food.

This pie is simply splendid, a unique dish to serve when company's coming and it will certainly appeal to everyone's palate.

Cheesy Potato Pie

Overall timing: 6-7 hours   Serves: 6-8

Butter Crunch Shell:

2 cups	crushed rice cereal	500 mL
1 cup	crushed All-Bran	250 mL
½ cup	melted butter	125 mL

Cheese and Potato Filling:

2 cups	cottage cheese	500 mL
2 cups	leftover mashed potatoes	500 mL
½ cup	sour cream	125 mL
1 tsp.	salt	5 mL
½ tsp.	freshly ground pepper	2 mL
½ tsp.	fine dill weed	2 mL
1 tbsp.	finely chopped green pepper	15 mL
½	green pepper, cut into strips	½

Mix cereals with melted butter. Press all but ½ cup (125 mL) into a 10" (25 mL) pie plate. Bake at 400°F (200°C) for 6-8 minutes, until it is lightly browned.

Beat together all filling ingredients, spoon into the shell. Spoon remaining ½ cup (125 mL) butter crunch mixture around edge of shell. Refrigerate 6 hours or overnight. Let sit at room temperature for ½ hour. Heat oven to 400°F (200°C) and bake for 20-25 minutes. Garnish with strips of green pepper. Serve hot.

It is interesting to note, that the first potatoes reached the Americas through English colonists who spent time in Bermuda, where they restocked their supplies. Although American Indians claimed to gather wild potatoes as far north as Nebraska, I am left with a question. Were the "wild potatoes" which the Indians of North America gathered, originally from Peruvian Stock? A fascinating history surrounds the potato.

Escalloped Potatoes and Barbecue Franks

Overall timing: 1 hour   *Serves: 4-6*

4-6	all-purpose potatoes, scrubbed, sliced	4-6
1 cup	diced celery	250 mL
2 tbsp.	butter	25 mL
3 tbsp.	flour	45 mL
2 tsp.	prepared mustard, Dijon style	10 mL
1 tsp.	salt	5 mL
2 cups	milk	250 mL
1 dozen	barbecue franks or European wieners	1 dozen

Layer potato slices and diced celery in an 8-cup (2 L) casserole. Melt butter in a saucepan, blend in flour, mustard, salt, add milk gradually. Heat until sauce boils. Pour over ingredients in casserole and bake at 400°F (200°C) for 45 minutes. Meanwhile, score and brown franks in a frying pan, place on top of escalloped potatoes to serve. Pass the hot Dijon mustard.

Chicken Hash

Overall timing: 45 minutes   *Serves: 4-6*

2 cups	boiling potatoes peeled, diced	500 mL
2 cups	chopped cooked chicken	500 mL
2 tbsp.	chicken fat or butter	25 mL
1 tbsp.	freshly chopped parsley	15 mL
½ tsp.	salt	2 mL
¼ tsp.	freshly ground pepper	1 mL
½-1 cup	chicken stock	125-250 mL

Prepare potatoes, boil and drain. Mix potatoes and chicken. Melt fat in frying pan and add potato mixture along with parsley, salt, pepper, and stock. Cook until browned, about 15 minutes. Serve hot with cranberry sauce.

This luncheon dish is extremely tasty. The combination of potatoes and fish has long been a staple in many countries.

Sea Scallop Potatoes

Overall timing: 1 hour, 20 minutes   Serves: 6-8

4	large, boiling potatoes, peeled, sliced	4
1 cup	cooked tuna, shrimp, or crab	250 mL
1	onion, chopped	1
1 tsp.	paprika	5 mL
1 tsp.	salt	5 mL
¼ tsp.	freshly ground pepper	1 mL
1 cup	cream	250 mL
¼-½ cup	white wine	50-125 mL
1 cup	cooked mushrooms	250 mL

In buttered 3-quart (3 L) casserole, place alternate layers of potatoes, fish, onion, salt, pepper, and paprika. Repeat layers. Combine cream, wine and mushrooms, heat and pour over all. Bake at 400°F for 1 hour and 10 minutes or until fork tender, when tested. Top with a dollop of butter and a sprig of parsley.

Potatoes, Hominy, and Onion Sauté

Overall timing: 45 minutes   Serves: 6

4-5	large, boiling potatoes, washed, diced	4-5
6	slices bacon, chopped	6
2	medium onions, chopped	2
1 cup	hominy (dry corn, coarsley ground)	250 mL
½ tsp.	salt	2 mL
¼ tsp.	freshly ground pepper	1 mL
½ cup	green onion, chopped	125 mL

Prepare and cook potatoes. In a heavy skillet fry bacon and cook onions, slowly, until soft. Add potatoes, hominy, salt, and pepper to bacon mixture and cook over moderate heat until vegetables are slightly browned, stirring occasionally. Sprinkle with green onion to serve.

Creamed Mushroom and Wine Potatoes

Overall timing: 1 hour, 20 minutes; 25 minutes microwaved   *Serves: 6*

3	*large baking potatoes, washed*	*3*
2	*onions, chopped*	*2*
4 tbsp.	*butter*	*60 mL*
2 cups	*sliced fresh mushrooms*	*500 mL*
½ cup	*white wine*	*125 mL*
1-2 tbsp.	*flour*	*15-25 mL*
1 cup	*sour cream*	*250 mL*

Bake potatoes. Sauté onions in butter until soft, add mushrooms, cook until soft, 5 minutes. Add wine, take off heat. Sprinkle flour over, stir to blend, put on the heat again and almost bring to a boil. Just before serving, halve the baked potatoes, cutting or slashing through the top, and place on individual serving plates. Add sour cream to mushroom and wine sauce, heat, do not boil, and pour over baked potatoes. Serve with rounds of buttered toast and cherry tomatoes.

 King Louis XVI was presented a potato blossom bouquet by potato crusader, Auguste Parmentier, and Queen Marie Antoinette wore a potato blossom in her hair. The affair they attended was a 10-course potato dish feast. One dish must have been a potato soufflé. . . .

Potatoes Soufflé

Overall timing: 1 hour   Serves: 4

2 cups	*hot mashed potatoes (3 large)*	*500 mL*
¼ cup	*chicken broth*	*50 mL*
2	*large eggs, separated*	*2*
1 tsp.	*salt*	*5 mL*
1½ cups	*cream*	*375 mL*

Peel potatoes and cook in a small amount of water. Drain. Mash. Combine hot potatoes with chicken broth, beaten egg yolks, salt, and cream. Fold in stiffly beaten egg whites. Mix lightly, pile into a greased 2-quart (2 L) dish. Place in a pan of hot water, and bake at 325°F (160°C) for 25-30 minutes. Serve immediately.

Mock Scallops

Overall timing: 45 minutes   Serves: 4-6

2 cups	mashed potatoes (may be leftovers)	500 mL
1½ cups	salt cod	375 mL
2	eggs, well beaten	2
½ cup	dry bread crumbs	125 mL

Prepare mashed potatoes. Shred salt cod, wash several times in fresh cold water. Cover with fresh cold water and bring to a boil. Pour off water and repeat the operation, depending on the amount of salt in the fish. (Do not cut dried salt fish with a steel knife as the fish will have a "steely" taste to it.) To freshened cod, add potatoes and eggs. Mix well. Shape into pieces the size of scallops and roll in bread crumbs. Fry in hot fat at 375°F (190°C) until brown. Serve with White Wine-Hollandaise Sauce below.

White Wine-Hollandaise

Makes: 1½ cups

¾ cup	butter	175 mL
⅓ cup	dry white wine	75 mL
2 tsp.	minced shallots	10 mL
½ tsp.	salt	2 mL
⅛ tsp.	freshly ground pepper	0.5 mL
1 tbsp.	cold water	15 mL
4	egg yolks	4
½-1 tsp.	lemon juice	2-5 mL
	cayenne to taste	

Have butter, at room temperature, then cut into small pieces (about 12 pieces). In a small saucepan combine wine, shallots, salt, and pepper. Reduce the liquid over high heat to about 2 tablespoons (25 mL). Remove the pot from the heat and add cold water. Add egg yolks, lightly beaten, and whisk the mixture until it is thick. Whisk in butter, 1 piece at a time, over low heat, lifting the pot occasionally to cool the mixture and making certain that each piece of butter is melted before adding more. Continue to whisk the sauce until it is thick and add lemon juice, and cayenne to taste. (Careful with the cayenne.)

Keep sauce warm, covered with a round of wax paper, in a shallow pan of warm water until ready to use.

Hot Tarragon Potatoes

Overall timing: 3 hours   Serves: 8

4-5	medium all-purpose potatoes, peeled, diced cooked	4-5
3 tbsp.	butter	45 mL
3 tbsp.	flour	45 mL
1 cup	light cream	250 mL
½ tsp.	salt	2 mL
½ tsp.	freshly ground pepper	2 mL
1 tbsp.	tarragon	15 mL
½ cup	grated Parmesan cheese	125 mL
1 cup	grated sharp Cheddar cheese	250 mL

Make a thick white sauce of butter, flour, and cream. When it comes to a boil take from heat, add salt, pepper, tarragon, Parmesan cheese, and stir in cooked potatoes. Cook another 5 minutes, to heat. Turn potato mixture into a well-greased ring mold, press down firmly, refrigerate for several hours or overnight.

A half hour before serving, turn potato ring out onto an ovenproof platter, bake at 400°F (200°C) for 30 minutes. In the last 5 minutes, sprinkle with Cheddar cheese, heat until cheese melts, serve hot.

Japanese Tofu Casserole

Overall timing: 45 minutes   Serves: 4-6

½ lb.	fresh or tinned tofu (soy bean curd)	250 g
2	onions, chopped	2
1 cup	finely chopped fresh mushrooms	250 mL
1 cup	chopped cooked potatoes, (may be leftovers)	250 mL
3	medium carrots, peeled, finely chopped	3
½ cup	raw or frozen peas	125 mL
5	eggs	5
1 tbsp.	ground ginger	15 mL
1 tsp.	salt	5 mL
2 tsp.	soy sauce	10 mL

Slice tofu, place in buttered flat baking dish. Sprinkle with chopped vegetables. Beat eggs with ginger, salt and soy sauce, pour over other ingredients in baking dish, stir lightly. Bake at 375°F (190°C) until it forms a golden brown crust, 20-30 minutes. Serve hot with salad.

When I was a youngster, picnics and potato salad were synonymous. Many a bucketful made its way to the Toews family gatherings at beautiful Cultus Lake, B.C.

The potato salad was lovingly loaded with eggs and creamy mayonnaise, seasoned with a good bunch of onion and salt and pepper. Mother always took great care to decorate it. Tomatoes became flowers, cucumbers became leaves, and fresh parsley always trimmed the top!

Old-Fashioned Potato Salad

Overall timing: 4 hours   Serves: 8-10

7	**all-purpose potatoes, pared, sliced**	7
⅓ cup	**Italian dressing**	75 mL
¾ cup	**sliced celery**	175 mL
⅓ cup	**sliced green onion tops**	75 mL
5	**hard-cooked eggs**	5
1 cup	**mayonnaise**	250 mL
½ cup	**sour cream**	125 mL
1½ tsp.	**horseradish/mustard mixed**	7 mL
1 tsp.	**salt**	5 mL
½ tsp.	**freshly ground pepper**	2 mL
1 tsp.	**celery seed (optional)**	5 mL

Boil potatoes in a small amount of water. Drain. Pour Italian dressing over warm potatoes; chill 2 hours. Then add celery and onion. Add chopped egg whites. Sieve egg yolks, mix with mayonnaise, sour cream, horseradish mustard and fold into salad. Add salt, pepper, and celery seed. Chill 2 hours, garnish with tomato and cucumber to serve, and trim with sprigs of fresh parsley.

Initially, the potato suffered rejection in Europe. It was pooh poohed and eyed with suspicion by Europeans for centuries, mostly because it was related to the deadly nightshade and mandrake plant. The Scots refused to eat it because it was not specifically mentioned in the Bible. Until the 19th Century, the English believed the potato to have unwholesome aphrodisiac effects.

Deluxe Potato Vegetable Salad

4-5	*all-purpose potatoes, pared, diced*	*4-5*
1	*small onion, chopped*	*1*
1 cup	*chopped cucumber*	*250 mL*
2 tbsp.	*grated Cheddar cheese*	*25 mL*
½ cup	*deviled ham*	*125 mL*
1	*10" (25 cm) celery stalk, diced*	*1*
1	*carrot, chopped, cooked*	*1*
20	*slices ham roll*	*20*

Dressing:

1 tbsp.	*vinegar*	*15 mL*
1 tbsp.	*sugar*	*15 mL*
½ tsp.	*salt*	*2 mL*
1 tbsp.	*sweet pickle juice*	*15 mL*
2 tbsp.	*mayonnaise*	*25 mL*
2 tbsp.	*sweet cream*	*25 mL*

Cook potatoes in a small amount of water, Drain, cool potatoes before tossing with other salad ingredients. Combine dressing ingredients, stir into salad. In a bread loaf pan, place slices of ham roll to cover bottom and sides. Press potato salad into loaf pan (mixture will be quite thick), cover with remaining ham roll slices. Refrigerate until serving time.

To serve, unmold onto an oblong platter, garnish with frosted grapes, radish flowers.

For frosted grapes, simply dip wet grapes into icing sugar.

For radish flowers, cut radish in half, cut into sides at an angle and cut back the angles carefully.

The Soviet Union and Europe grow 75 percent of the world's potato crop. In a very good year the Russians, who call potatoes their second bread, are credited for one-third of world production.

Potato Sauerkraut Salad

6	medium, new potatoes, washed, quartered, sliced	6
1 tbsp.	minced onion	15 mL
½	green pepper, minced	½
1 tbsp.	freshly chopped parsley	15 mL
2 tbsp.	freshly chopped watercress	25 mL
1 cup	sauerkraut	250 mL
¼ cup	sweet cream	50 mL
½ cup	mayonnaise	125 mL
½ tsp.	salt	2 mL
½ tsp.	freshly ground pepper	2 mL
¼ cup	pimiento, minced	50 mL

Cook potatoes in a small amount of water. Drain and cool. You may place on a flat platter and refrigerate to speed cooling. Combine potatoes, onion, green pepper, parsley, watercress, sauerkraut. Chill for 1 hour. Before serving, beat cream with mayonnaise, salt, pepper, pimiento, pour dressing over salad, mixing lightly. Sprinkle with a little more pimiento to serve.

Three Cheese Potato Salad

Overall timing: 2 hours, 40 minutes   Serves: 4-6

4	boiling potatoes, pared, diced	4
½ tsp.	salt	2 mL
¼ tsp.	freshly ground pepper	1 mL
6 oz.	small curd cottage cheese	170 g
3 oz.	pkg. cream cheese	85 g
1 cup	diagonally chopped celery	250 mL
2-4 oz.	blue cheese, crumbled	55-115 g

Cook potatoes in a small amount of water. Drain. Sprinkle with salt and pepper, cool. Mash or beat together cottage cheese and cream cheese until smooth and creamy. When potatoes are cold, mix them together with cottage cheese mixture and celery. Stir in blue cheese. Chill 2 hours. Trim with parsley and chopped chives.

Russian Pickle Salad

Overall timing: 1 hour   Serves: 6-8

2	chicken breasts, cooked, skinned, diced	2
4	boiling potatoes, peeled, diced, cooked	4
3	hard-cooked eggs, chopped	3
3	dill pickles, chopped	3
1½ cups	sour cream	375 mL
1 tsp.	dill seed	5 mL
1 tbsp.	vinegar	15 mL
1 tsp.	oregano	5 mL
	salt, pepper	
⅛ tsp.	sherry pepper sauce	0.5 mL

When chicken, potatoes, and eggs are cooked and cooled, mix lightly with other ingredients. Chill before serving, garnish with dill.

Rich Potato Salad

Overall timing: 3 hours   Serves: 8

8	medium potatoes (your preference)	8
7	egg yolks, beaten	7
1 cup	cider vinegar	250 mL
5 tbsp.	sugar	75 mL
1 tbsp.	dry mustard	15 mL
2 tsp.	salt	10 mL
2 tbsp.	butter	25 mL
1½ cups	sour cream	375 mL
¼ tsp.	freshly ground pepper	1 mL
⅓ cup	whipping cream	75 mL

Peel potatoes and boil in a small amount of water until tender. Drain. Refrigerate until cool, 1 hour, in a glass bowl. In double boiler saucepan, combine egg yolks, vinegar, sugar, mustard, 1 tsp. (5 mL) of the salt, and bring to a boil, cook, stirring constantly until very thick, 8-10 minutes. Remove from heat, add butter, let cool. When cold add sour cream, combine well. Season potatoes with other tsp. (5 mL) salt and the pepper. Add dressing and whipping cream, stirring gently. Chill, covered.

Serve in a lettuce-lined bowl, garnish and dust with paprika.

Mussel farming started in P.E.I. in 1978. Cultured mussels are plump and grit-free and are generally available in major centers.

We have gathered mussels on the Sunshine Coast, B.C., and on the beaches and rocky areas of Oregon and California waters. They are plentiful but small!

Mussel and Potato Salad
I

Overall timing: 2 hours   Serves: 4 as main course, 8 as first course

4	*large new potatoes, washed, diced*	4
⅓ cup	*tomato paste*	75 mL
1½ cups	*mayonnaise*	375 ML
1	*minced red pepper*	1
½ tsp.	*chopped chives*	2 mL
2 tbsp.	*white wine*	25 mL
4 lbs.	*mussels, cleaned, steamed open, shelled (5-8 minutes) discard unopened mussels*	2 kg
2	*hard-cooked eggs*	2
½ lb.	*whole blanched green beans mussel shells*	250 g

Cook potatoes until just tender, cool. Fold the tomato paste into mayonnaise with red pepper, chives, and white wine. In a large bowl, toss mussels with tomato, mayonnaise and potatoes. Serve in large oyster or clam shells. Garnish creatively with eggs, beans, and a few mussel shells.

Mussel and Potato Salad
II

Substitute ¼ cup (50 mL) sour cream for tomato paste and ½ of a minced green pepper for minced red pepper.

Garnish with parsley, lettuce, lemon and egg slices, and a few mussel shells.

See photograph on front cover.

An aspic is a crystal clear jellied dish with three uses, in this case for making a mold in which potato salad is encased. There is beauty and snappy flavor in a shimmering aspic! This is a sight to see on a summer buffet table.

Potato Salad in Aspic

Overall timing: 3 hours   *Serves: 8-10*

2 cups	*potato salad*	*500 mL*
4 cups	*tomato juice*	*1 L*
2 x 7 oz.	*pkgs. aspic tomato gelatin*	*2*
	tomato slices	
½ cup	*celery slices*	*125 mL*
	lettuce leaves	

Oil a 6-8 cup (1.5-2 L) mold. Heat to boiling, 2 cups (500 mL) of tomato juice, add aspic gelatin, stir to dissolve, then add and stir well remaining 2 cups (500 mL) tomato juice. Pour ½ of the gelatin mixture into an oiled mold. When partially set, arrange slices of tomato in center of salad with celery slices around the rim pushing them down to the bottom of the mold. When set, add a layer of potato salad, and pour remaining aspic on top. Chill until firm, approximately 2 hours.

Arrange lettuce leaves on a dish to fit the mold and unmold aspic, carefully onto it to serve. Before serving, you may garnish with small rosettes of salad dressing.

Nutritionists rate the quality of protein of the potato higher than that of the soybean.

Italian Green Bean and Potato Salad

Overall timing: *6 hours or overnight*   Serves: *6-8*

4	*large, all-purpose potatoes, pared, diced*	4
2 cups	*chopped fresh green beans*	500 mL
2	*onions, chopped*	2
2 tbsp.	*olive oil*	25 mL
1 tbsp.	*wine vinegar*	15 mL

Cook potatoes and green beans and cool. Toss gently with onions, salt, and freshly ground pepper. Add oil and vinegar, stir gently. Marinate in refrigerator. Stir gently before serving and taste! Add another tablespoon (15 mL) of vinegar for more tang!

Jicama potatoes are grown in Mexico and must be eaten raw. They look somewhat like yams and must be peeled. They are available in the supermarket from May to July, are economical to buy, and have a flavor somewhat like a mild radish.

Jicama Potato Slaw

Overall timing: *15 minutes*   Serves: *6-8*

1	*4" x 4" jicama potato, peeled, grated raw*	1
2 tbsp.	*mayonnaise*	25 mL
3	*green onions, chopped*	3

Mix all ingredients, serve immediately or refrigerate. This salad may be kept refrigerated for several days.

Common garden weeds, and we have approximately 40 species in Canada, are not only fun and interesting, but valuable to you financially and nutritionally. Would you believe that most common weeds are unsurpassed in vitamins, protein and mineral content when compared to most common salad greens, such as celery, onions, lettuce, spinach?

"Weedy salads" are springing up all over Canada. Not to let weed eaters feel left out, I have included two recipes which I think you will agree add a novel and gourmet touch to this collection of nutritious and low-cost potato recipes.

Red and white clover is known to almost everyone. Clover belongs to the pea family, true clover having three leaves. Clover was introduced into North America from Europe as a crop plant, and eventually escaped from tended gardens and fields to maintain a footing almost everywhere. Most of us can remember happy childhood days spent searching for four leafed clovers.

Potato-Clover Salad

Overall timing: 3 hours   Serves: 2

2 cups	**washed and chopped young clover leaves**	500 mL
2 cups	**cubed cooked boiling potatoes, cooled**	500 mL
½ cup	**sliced fresh raw mushrooms**	125 mL
1	**stalk celery, thinly sliced**	1
1	**onion, diced**	1
6	**slices bacon, cooked crisp, crumbled (optional)**	6
	salt and pepper to taste	
2 tbsp.	**olive oil**	25 mL
2 tbsp.	**wine or cider vinegar**	25 mL
1 tsp.	**sugar**	5 mL
	grated Romano cheese	

In a salad bowl, combine clover leaves, potatoes, mushrooms, celery, onion and bacon. Add seasonings, olive oil, vinegar and sugar. Toss well and sprinkle with Romano cheese. Chill 2 hours before serving.

In boiling or baking unpeeled potatoes there is little or no loss of vitamin C or other nutrients. The potato has a unique capacity to increase vitamin C in storage. It is possible that this vitamin C is developed for use in metabolism by the tuber (Franke 1960). Potatoes used most often should be organically grown heritage potatoes, cooked with skins on because this method retains the delicate slightly sweet flavour of the potato.

For use in Potato Tortillas Tapas–Spain, page 6.

Spicy Lentil Salad

1 cup	*green or brown lentils*	*250 mL*
½ cup	*chopped onion*	*125 mL*
2	*tomatoes, chopped*	*2*
¼ cup	*organic olive oil*	*75 mL*
2 tsp.	*cumin*	*10 mL*
1 tsp.	*hot pepper sauce or more to taste*	*5 mL*
1 tsp.	*Celtic sea salt*	*5 mL*
3-4	*garlic cloves, crushed*	*3-4*

Wash and boil lentils in 2 cups (500 mL) water until done, about 30 minutes. Drain. Add other ingredients and keep warm. Spoon into potato tortillas and use as directed, see page 6.

The University of Guelph in Ontario reports that department of molecular biology and genetic scientists are working to develop a detection method for verticillium fungus which causes what's known as "early dying syndrome in potatoes". Half of Ontario's (province of Canada) potato crop is lost due to this challenge. The most effective pesticide has been banned in Canada. Infected plants are characterized by stunted growth and wilting leaves, followed by yellowing and eventual plant death. The verticillium, which is a soil-bound pathogen, along with a nematode work together to cause the disease. The new method for detection is based on molecular genetics and the impact of this technology will be felt not only in Ontario, but also on national and global levels, reports Prof. Jane Robb (Mar. 2000).

Manitoba's soil is rich in minerals and summer rains are abundant. The days are long and hot, followed by cool nights, and seem to produce fantastic potatoes — reds and the famous Russet Burbanks. Potatoes are Manitoba's No. 1 vegetable crop. Washington and Idaho States, south of the border, share the same honors.

Hot German Potato Salad with Asparagus

Overall timing: 1 hour   Serves: 6-8 (Completed on the barbecue)

1 lb.	*asparagus, cleaned, cut into 1" (2.5 cm) pieces*	*500 g*
6	*large baking potatoes, washed, cubed*	*6*
8	*rashers bacon*	*8*
1 cup	*chopped celery*	*250 mL*
3	*green onions, chopped*	*3*
½ cup	*mayonnaise*	*125 mL*
¼ cup	*white vinegar*	*50 mL*
2 tsp.	*white sugar*	*10 mL*
1 tsp.	*salt*	*5 mL*
1 tsp.	*dry mustard*	*5 mL*
¼ tsp.	*freshly ground pepper*	*1 mL*

Cook asparagus and potatoes separately in boiling water just until tender. In a large bowl, combine potatoes, asparagus. Fry bacon, crumble. Add bacon bits, celery, and onion to potato mixture. Combine remaining ingredients and pour over potatoes, toss well.

Wrap salad securely in double thickness of heavy-duty tin foil. Place on barbecue grill 4" (10 cm) from heat, cook for 25 minutes.

In the Philippines, four centuries after Spanish introduction, potatoes are still a luxury dish. Philippine housewives place potatoes on top of the shopping cart, to show that they are a family of means.

Hot Sausage and Potato Salad

Overall timing: 55 minutes   *Serves: 6-8*

6	medium, boiling potatoes, scrubbed, sliced	6
1 lb.	pork sausage meat	500 g
1	onion	1
½ cup	white wine vinegar	125 mL
½ cup	water	125 mL
1½ tsp.	dry mustard powder	7 mL
½ tsp.	salt	2 mL
1 tsp.	thyme	5 mL
½ tsp.	freshly ground pepper	2 mL
1 tbsp.	chopped fresh chives	15 mL

Cook potatoes until fork tender. Meanwhile, brown sausage meat in frying pan. Drain potatoes. Spoon sausage meat into potatoes, leaving fat and drippings in frying pan. Keep potato mixture hot. Chop onion and add to fat in frying pan along with vinegar, water, mustard, salt, thyme, pepper and bring to a boil. Pour over potatoes, tossing gently, sprinkle with chives. Serve with crusty buttered French bread.

Brightly hued 2-storey houses, where the kitchen was an open forum for whomever may drop in, were a familiar sight in Newfoundland at the turn of the '50's decade. The sheep and cows and goats wandered. In those days, the house was surrounded by a white picket fence, which protected the POTATO patch! A fence to keep the animals out.

In Tubingen, West Germany, genetic engineers have fused two botanical cousins, the tomato and potato. They have produced, topatoes, and pomatoes. These scientists are hoping that someday the hybrids will produce food above and below the ground!

Serve the cousins together occasionally.

Hot German Kartoffel

Overall timing: 30 minutes   *Serves: 4-6*

4	medium boiling potatoes, washed, diced	4
4	strips bacon	4
1	onion, chopped	1
2	dill pickles, chopped	2
¼ cup	chicken stock	50 mL
¼ cup	vinegar	50 mL
1 tsp.	sugar	5 mL
½ tsp.	salt	2 mL
¼ tsp.	dry mustard	1 mL
1 tbsp.	minced parsley	15 mL

Prepare and cook potatoes, drain. Keep hot. Chop bacon and cook in a skillet together with onion, dill pickle, stock, vinegar, sugar, and spices. Heat to boiling. Return potatoes to skillet, stirring gently, then serve. Nice with pumpernickel or rye bread, and German tomato salad.

Fish and Potato Salad

Substitute 1 lb. (500 g) fresh boneless whitefish, cut into 2" (5 cm) pieces, for bacon. Also substitute 2 large stalks celery for dill pickle. Discard celery after cooking. Serve warm.

What do you think has made the almighty potato King among vegetables? Nutritiousness, hardiness, fruitfulness, that's what, and versatility! That is why a jack-of-all-trades, in India, is called "alu" or potato.

Hot Potato Salad-Alu Chat

Overall timing: 30 minutes   Serves: 8

6	**boiling potatoes, scrubbed, diced**	6
1 cup	**minced lamb, or cooked, chopped, leftover lamb**	250 mL
1 cup	**chopped scallions**	250 mL
1 cup	**fresh peas**	250 mL
1 tsp.	**dried mango powder (specialty shop)**	5 mL
1 tsp.	**coriander seed**	5 mL
½ tsp.	**tamarind (specialty shop)**	2 mL
1 cup	**mayonnaise**	250 mL
½ cup	**yogurt**	125 mL

Cook potatoes, drain, keep hot. Meanwhile, cook minced lamb, scallions, and peas with spices. Simmer 10 minutes, then add mayonnaise and yogurt. Heat and pour over potatoes, mix gently and serve hot. This is nice served in pita bread.

Because the potato is of the botanical family of hallucinogenic and narcotic plants, such as deadly nightshade and mandrake, law-abiding Europeans wanted no such "ride with the devil", and shunned the nutritious potato, along with another member of the family, the tomato, until the 19th Century.

DINNER AND SIDE DISHES

Did you know that potatoes are produced in 130 of the world's 167 independent countries? One year's crop is worth approximately 106 billion dollars! Without potatoes, meat production would fall and the price of meat would skyrocket, because almost half of the world's crop of potatoes is fed to livestock.

In this section you will discover the old and the new, the classics, the contemporary, and lots of good honest flavors in meat and potato dishes, a sensible, nutritious, contemporary combination.
Let's begin with Shepherd's pie.

Shepherd's Pie

Overall timing: 30 minutes   *Serves: 6*

1 tbsp.	*butter*	*15 mL*
2 cups	*chopped, leftover beef, lamb, or pork*	*500 mL*
2 tbsp.	*flour*	*25 mL*
¼ tsp.	*allspice*	*1 mL*
1½ cups	*leftover vegetables*	*375 mL*
1 cup	*leftover gravy*	*250 mL*
2 cups	*leftover mashed potatoes*	*500 mL*
½ cup	*cream*	*125 mL*
1	*egg, beaten*	*1*

Butter a 2-3 quart (2-3 L) baking dish, depending on amount of leftovers. Dice meat and stir in flour, allspice, and vegetables. At this point, add any gravy that may have been leftover. Pour into baking dish.

Combine potatoes and cream. Cover meat mixture with the mashed potatoes. Brush top with beaten egg and bake at 400°F (200°C) for 20 minutes.

Variation:
— Prepare a pastry crust and place into dish. Add filling, top with potatoes, bake as above, adding 20 minutes to cooking time.

The potato, native South American, praised for its versatility and nutrition, grows in more countries now than any other crop, except corn. Adaptable and hardy, the potato grows from below sea level, behind Dutch dikes, to 14,000 feet (4300 m) up in the Andes and Himalayas, and in the scorching deserts of Australia and Africa. Only jungle areas where humidity is high, and wilt and disease are encouraged, are not conducive to potato culture. Perhaps if world temperature drops, as climatologists predict, the almighty potato will become a crop of even greater importance.

Konigsberger Meatballs

Overall timing: 30 minutes   *Serves: 6*

1 lb.	ground beef	500 g
1 lb.	ground pork	500 g
1 cup	leftover mashed potatoes	250 mL
1 cup	bread crumbs	250 mL
1 tsp.	anchovy paste	5 mL
1	egg	1
1 tsp.	salt	5 mL
1 tsp.	freshly ground pepper	5 mL
	flour	

Sauce:

2 tbsp.	butter	25 mL
2 tbsp.	flour	25 mL
1 cup	potato water	250 mL
2	beef bouillon cubes	2
1 tbsp.	chopped fresh parsley	15 mL
1 tsp.	lemon juice	5 mL
1 tbsp.	capers	15 mL

Mix meat mixture thoroughly and shape into 2" (5 cm) balls. Dredge them in flour. Drop into a Dutch oven full of boiling salted water, cover and simmer for 15 minutes. Drain. (Save water for soup).

For sauce, melt butter in a saucepan. Stir in flour. Add water, bouillon cubes, parsley, lemon juice, and capers. Simmer for 5 minutes, then pour over meatballs to serve. Nice with sauerkraut and salad.

Although Philippine farmers are getting support from the International Potato Center, in Lima, Peru, potatoes are still considered a rich man's food in poor nations. This internationally funded center, founded in 1971, helps adapt potato cultivation to diverse regions and researchers are still drawing from South American stock. Experimentation with potatoes from seed is currently in progress and the potato is being seriously considered as a possible solution to world hunger.

Because potatoes grown in the Andes of Peru attain such a range of shapes and colors, the Quechua Indian language offers at least a thousand words for them! Each potato has a name and they are often creative and humorous. Names such as "cat's nose", and "potato makes young bride weep", and "pigs dropping" are popular.

Peruvian Potato Hamburger Casserole

Overall timing: 2 hours, 30 minutes   *Serves: 6-8*

6	raw potatoes, pared, sliced	6
1	sliced onion	1
4 cups	raw ground beef	1 L
1 cup	chopped celery	250 mL
1	minced green pepper	1
2 tsp.	salt	10 mL
⅛ tsp.	sherry peppers sauce	0.5 mL
½ tsp.	crushed garlic	2 mL
3-4	green pepper rings	3-4

Place potatoes in a 8-cup (2 L) greased roaster or casserole. Sprinkle with sliced onion, reserving half for the top. Mix raw ground beef, celery, green pepper, salt, and pepper sauce, and garlic. Place on top of the potatoes. Add tomatoes, letting juice run through, but do not stir. Garnish with rest of onion and green pepper rings. Cover and bake 1½-2 hours at 350°F (180°C).

Potato Chili (Pouce Coupé)

Overall timing: 1 hour, 30 minutes   *Serves: 6*

2 tbsp.	olive oil	25 mL
1	large onion, chopped	1
1	green pepper, chopped	1
1 lb.	ground beef	500 g
2 cups	canned tomatoes	500 mL
6 oz.	tomato paste	170 g
1 tsp.	Dijon mustard	5 mL
3 tbsp.	molasses	45 mL
⅛ tsp.	cayenne pepper	0.5 mL

Potato Chili (Pouce Coupé) (cont'd)

1	bay leaf	1
2 tsp.	finely chopped, seeded, fresh, red or green hot chilis	10 mL
1 tsp.	tumeric	5 mL
1 tsp.	salt	5 mL
1½ cups	cooked kidney beans	375 mL
3	boiled potatoes, chopped	3

Heat oil in a 10" (25 cm) skillet. Add onion, green pepper, ground beef. Cook until brown, stirring, then add next 7 ingredients. Put into casserole and bake at 400°F (200°C) for an hour, stirring occasionally. Add ½ cup (125 mL) red wine or water if mixture gets too thick. Combine last 4 ingredients, toss well, and add to meat mixture. Heat through. Serve with corn bread and a tossed salad.

Red Flannel Derry Hash originated in New Hampshire, where Daniel Webster once exclaimed, "God Almight makes men!" He seemed to have been overwhelmed by the rugged grandeur of that state. Along with potatoes, salt pork, and tripe, one finds dishes here like maple custard and "Newton" sugar squares.

A flavorful hash which you fold as an omelet, it is red because of the beets.

Red Flannel Derry Hash

Overall timing: 40 minutes   Serves: 4-6

2 cups	chopped, cooked corned beef	500 mL
2 cups	chopped, cooked beets	500 mL
4 cups	chopped, cooked boiling potatoes	1 L
1	large onion, chopped	1
1 tsp.	salt	5 mL
½ tsp.	freshly ground pepper	2 mL
½ cup	light cream	125 mL
¼ cup	bacon or pork drippings	50 mL
1 tbsp.	chopped fresh parsley	15 mL

Combine beef with beets, potatoes, onion, seasonings and cream. Heat bacon fat in a large skillet. Spoon mixture into skillet and spread evenly. Cook over low heat, without stirring, until bottom is well crusted. Fold as an omelet, serve immediately, sprinkled with parsley.

Where the raw potato is grated into the meat.

Potato Burgers

Overall timing: 45 minutes   Serves: 6

2 cups	raw, shredded, boiling potatoes	500 mL
2 lbs.	lean ground beef	1 kg
3	eggs, slightly beaten	3
1	onion, chopped	1
½	green pepper, chopped	½
1 tsp.	salt	5 mL
½ tsp.	freshly ground pepper	2 mL
½ tsp.	sherry pepper sauce	2 mL

Combine potatoes, ground beef, eggs, onion, green peppers, salt, pepper, sherry pepper sauce. Shape into 12 patties, ½" (1.3 cm) thick. Fry in a small amount of oil on low heat in a covered pan, 3-4 minutes on each side. Uncover, increase heat and continue cooking for another 10 minutes, to brown. Serve with relish, pickles, lettuce and tomato on a warm kaiser roll, for a complete meal-in-one!

Variation: Deep-Fried Mennonite Katlettin

Overall timing: 30 minutes   Serves: 4

1	egg	1
½ cup	cream	125 mL
½ cup	bread crumbs	125 mL
1	medium dry potato	1
1 tsp.	salt	5 mL
⅛ tsp.	pepper	0.5 mL
½	minced green pepper (optional)	½
1½ lbs.	lean ground beef or pork	750 g

Chop all ingredients, except ground meat, in blender, then mix well with meat. Shape into 2" (5 cm) patties and deep-fry in hot fat at 375°F (190°C), turning until crisp, 3-5 minutes.

Southern Potato and Sparerib Bake

Overall timing: 3 hours   Serves: 6-8

6	large potatoes, scrubbed, sliced	6
6	small onions, sliced	6
4 lbs.	pork spareribs	2 kg
2 cups	tomato sauce	250 mL
½ cup	white wine	125 mL
¼ cup	vinegar	50 mL
3 tbsp.	brown sugar	45 mL
1 tbsp.	prepared mustard	15 mL
1 tbsp.	rosemary	15 mL

In a 7-8 cup (2 L) baking dish, place sliced potatoes and onions. Cover with spareribs which have been cut into chunks. Mix the rest of ingredients, bring to a boil and pour over spareribs. Cover and bake at 350°F (180°C) for about 2 hours. Remove some of the fat from dish at this point, if there is an excess. With lid off, place dish under broiler and brown meat.

Fiery Punjabi Curry

Overall timing: 2 hours, 30 minutes   Serves: 6-8

2 tbsp.	salad oil	25 mL
4	medium onions, chopped	4
6 oz.	can tomato paste	170 g
2 cups	water	500 mL
1 tsp.	garlic powder	5 mL
6 tbsp.	imported curry powder	90 mL
2 lbs.	boneless, beef, or lamb, cubed	1 kg
6	large boiling potatoes, peeled, cubed	6

Sauté onions lightly in oil, add tomato paste, water, garlic powder, curry powder and cook until mixture thickens. Add meat and simmer 1 hour. Add potatoes and simmer 1 hour. Add additional curry powder and water to desired consistency. Serve over hot rice with chutney.

Lancashire Hot-Pot

Overall timing: 3 hours   Serves: 4-6

2 lbs.	lamb	1 kg
2	lamb kidneys (optional)	2
5	baking potatoes	5
2	onions	2
1 tsp.	salt	5 mL
½ tsp.	white pepper	2 mL
1 tsp.	chopped mint	5 mL
1 cup	beef or lamb stock, hot	250 mL

Trim meat and kidneys. Cut into small pieces. Peel potatoes and slice about ¼" (1 cm) thick. Slice onions thinly. Put layers of meat and vegetables into a greased 3-quart (3 L) casserole. Season. Sprinkle with chopped mint. Add stock and cover casserole. Bake for 2½-3 hours at 350°F (180°C), removing lid last ½ hour to brown potatoes.

Bohemian Potato Nut Loaf

Overall timing: 1 hour, 30 minutes   Serves: 6-8

1 cup	ground lamb	250 mL
3 cups	mashed potatoes	750 mL
1 cup	diced celery	250 mL
2 cups	chopped nuts	500 mL
1	egg, beaten	1
2 tbsp.	melted butter	25 mL
2 tbsp.	chopped onion	25 mL
1 tsp.	salt	5 mL
1 tsp.	paprika	5 mL

Combine all ingredients. Mix well. Pack into 2 greased 9" x 5" x 2" (23 cm x 13 cm x 5 cm) loaf pans and bake at 375°F (190°C) for 1 hour or until center is done. Serve with Cheese and Tomato Sauce, see page 84.

Rhenish Potato and Ham

4 tbsp.	*unbleached white flour*	*60 mL*
8 tbsp.	*water*	*120 mL*
5	*eggs*	*5*
½ tsp.	*salt*	*2 mL*
¼ tsp.	*freshly ground pepper*	*1 mL*
¼ tsp.	*nutmeg*	*1 mL*
¼ tsp.	*crushed garlic*	*1 mL*
2 tbsp.	*butter*	*25 mL*
8	*large boiling potatoes, boiled, sliced*	*8*
1 cup	*ham cubes*	*250 mL*

Stir the flour into the water until a thick paste forms. Add eggs, salt, pepper, nutmeg, and garlic. Heat the butter in frying pan, cover the bottom with thick slices of potato. Pour on the batter, sprinkle with ham cubes, and sauté on both sides until golden brown.

Potato Meat Loaf

2 lbs.	*ground beef*	*1 kg*
½ cup	*rolled oats*	*125 mL*
1 tsp.	*salt*	*5 mL*
½ tsp.	*freshly ground pepper*	*2 mL*
1	*egg*	*1*
1 tsp.	*parsley*	*5 mL*
1 tsp.	*onion juice*	*5 mL*
½ cup	*milk*	*125 mL*
⅛ tsp.	*sherry peppers sauce*	*0.5 mL*
5	*medium potatoes, boiled, mashed*	*5*

Preheat oven to 400°F (260°C). Combine first 9 ingredients, mix thoroughly. Shape into 2 loaves approximately 3" x 8" (7 cm x 20 cm). Place on a cookie sheet and bake for 45 minutes. Meanwhile, make mashed potatoes. To serve, place half of mashed potatoes on first meat loaf, put on second layer of meat loaf and top with remaining mashed potatoes. Garnish with parsley.

"This potato tuna dish is sumptuous but simple and one can survive on it quite nicely! . . .

Potato Tuna Parmesan

Overall timing: 2 hours   Serves: 6

3 cups	*scrubbed, thinly sliced potatoes*	*750 mL*
¾ cup	*sliced onions*	*175 mL*
½ cup	*cooked tuna*	*125 mL*
½ cup	*sliced celery*	*125 mL*
½ cup	*cream*	*125 mL*
1 cup	*plain yogurt*	*250 mL*
1½ tbsp.	*flour*	*22 mL*
½ tsp.	*salt*	*2 mL*
½ cup	*grated Parmesan cheese*	*125 mL*
1 cup	*grated sharp Cheddar cheese*	*250 mL*

Butter a 2-quart (2 L) baking dish and in it alternate layers of potatoes, onions, tuna, celery. In bowl combine cream, yogurt, flour, salt, Parmesan cheese, and pour over all. Bake 1½ hours, sprinkle Cheddar cheese over top, return to the oven until cheese melts.

Cod and Potato Casserole with Cloves

Overall timing: 1 hour, 10 minutes   Serves: 6

2 lbs.	*fresh cod*	*1 kg*
4	*boiling potatoes, scrubbed, sliced*	*4*
2	*onions, sliced*	*2*
6	*whole cloves*	*6*
1	*bay leaf*	*1*
¼ tsp.	*dried dill seed*	*1 mL*
¼ tsp.	*salt*	*1 mL*
¼ tsp.	*white pepper*	*1 mL*
1 tbsp.	*butter*	*15 mL*
½ cup	*dry white wine*	*125 mL*
2 cups	*boiling water*	*500 mL*
1 cup	*scalded milk*	*250 mL*

Cod and Potato Casserole with Cloves (cont'd)

Butter a 2-3-quart (2-3 L) casserole. Preheat oven to 375°F (190°C). Place alternate layers of cod, potatoes, onions. Add all other ingredients except milk. Bake for 1 hour, covered. Before serving, remove bay leaf and cloves, then add scalded milk, stir gently and taste for seasoning.

Capetown Potato and Fish Stew

Overall timing: 1 hour   *Serves: 4-6*

1½ lbs.	fresh sole	750 g
½ tsp.	salt	2 mL
2 tbsp.	flour	25 mL
2 tbsp.	butter	25 mL
3	small onions, cubed	3
1 lb.	fresh green beans, chopped	500 g
6	medium boiling potatoes, peeled	6
4	fresh tomatoes	4
2	hot, red or green, chili peppers	2
1 cup	cauliflower chunks	250 mL
1 cup	fresh peas	250 mL
½ cup	water	125 mL
½	quince, cooked*	½
2 tbsp.	crumbled summer savory leaves	25 mL

Cut the sole into chunks, sprinkle with salt and flour, and brown in butter. Set aside. Combine all but sole, quince, and savory and boil gently ½ hour, or until vegetables are tender. Add sole, quince, and savory leaves. Heat. Accompany stew with buttered potatoes.

*The quince is the unusual ingredient, if not available you can substitute quince jelly, or a pear.

Hash is a combination of foods chopped into small pieces and seasoned. An excellent way to use leftovers.

Heavenly Hash

Overall timing: 30 minutes   Serves: 4-6

Fish:

2 cups	cooked, flaked fish	500 mL
3 cups	leftover mashed potatoes	750 mL
1	egg, beaten	1
½ tsp.	salt	2 mL
½ tsp.	white pepper	2 mL
1 tbsp.	butter	15 mL
1 tbsp.	minced onion	15 mL
12	rashers bacon, chopped	12

Cook potatoes if you do not have leftovers. Combine all ingredients except bacon. Fry bacon until crisp, then add potato and fish mixture, turning to brown on both sides. May be served like an omelet.

Corned Beef:

Substitute 1¼ cups (300 mL) finely chopped corned beef for cooked fish.

Frankfurter:

6	thinly sliced franks

Roast Beef:

1½ cups	(375 mL) finely chopped, cooked lean roast beef.

Lamb:

1½ cups	(375 mL) finely chopped, cooked lean lamb

78

The tools for harvesting potatoes in Peru have not changed since before Inca times! Many village farmers are surprised to have people come from other continents to learn about potatoes. They do not realize how important their potatoes have become in other lands.

The potato was once worshipped as a spirit by Peruvian Indians, Jugs and vessels have been found to be shaped like a potato, complete with indentations resembling the eyes on potatoes.

Sailor's Pie

Overall timing: 1 hour   *Serves: 6*

2	*large onions, sliced*	*2*
1 tbsp.	*fat*	*15 mL*
2 cups	*leftover mashed potatoes*	*500 mL*
2 cups	*minced, cooked clams*	*500 mL*
½ tsp.	*salt*	*2 mL*
½ tsp.	*freshly ground pepper*	*2 mL*
1 tbsp.	*chopped fresh parsley*	*15 mL*

Pastry:

½ tsp.	*salt*	*2 mL*
2 cups	*unbleached white flour*	*500 mL*
½ cup	*lard*	*125 mL*
2 tbsp.	*margarine*	*25 mL*
6-8 tbsp.	*water*	*90-120 mL*

Cook onions in fat until soft and brown. Add potatoes, clams, salt, pepper, and parsley. Heat, then pour into a 3-quart (3 L) baking dish. Make pastry by blending salt into flour then lard and margarine, mix until crumbly. Gently stir in water. Roll out pastry to fit baking dish. Place pastry over potato mixture, prick pastry to allow steam to escape. Bake at 400°F (200°C) for 35-40 minutes.

In the Netherlands, one fourth of all arable land is devoted to the growing of potatoes. The hardworking Dutch have expanded the potato export business into an export business worth more than their tulip industry!

Potato Salmon Puff

Overall timing: 1 hour   *Serves: 6*

4 cups	mashed potatoes	1 L
2 cups	flaked cooked salmon*	500 mL
3	egg yolks, beaten	3
1 tsp.	salt	5 mL
½ tsp.	freshly ground pepper	2 mL
1	onion, minced	1
1 tbsp.	minced fresh parsley	15 mL
3	egg white, stiffly beaten	3

Prepare potatoes if you haven't any leftovers. Mix together potatoes, salmon, egg yolks, salt, pepper, onion, and parsley. Fold in stiffly beaten egg whites. Pour into greased 3-quart (3 L) casserole and bake at 375°F (190°C) for 30 minutes. Serve immediately.

*You may use 1½ cups (375 ml) canned mackeral.

Basque Potato Casserole

Overall timing: 40 minutes   *Serves: 6*

5	medium boiling potatoes, pared, cooked, mashed	5
2 tbsp.	olive oil	25 mL
3	large onions, diced	3
4	cloves garlic, minced	4
6 oz.	jar pimiento, sliced, with liquid	170 g
½ cup	stuffed green olives, sliced	125 mL
5	tomatoes, skinned, chopped	5
¼ tsp.	freshly ground pepper	1 mL
½ tsp.	salt	2 mL
½ tsp.	basil	2 mL
¼ tsp.	oregano	1 mL
3 tbsp.	grated Parmesan cheese	45 mL

While potatoes are cooking, heat oil in a skillet, adding onion and garlic, cook until soft. Add pimientos, olives, tomatoes, pepper, salt, basil and oregano. Simmer, uncovered, for 5 minutes. Turn into a 9" (23 cm) pie plate. Drain and mash potatoes. Spoon into center of vegetable mixture, flatten slightly so that the sauce oozes around the potato. Sprinkle with cheese. Brown under the broiler, serve hot.

A vegetarian cutlet, with tarragon and shallots, prepared to perfection.

Vegetable Cutlets Béarnaise

Overall timing: 1 hour   Serves: 6-7

4	boiling potatoes, peeled, boiled and mashed	4
1 cup	chopped green pepper	250 mL
1 cup	grated raw carrot	250 mL
1 cup	chopped raw watercress	250 mL
1 cup	chopped raw spinach	250 mL
1 tbsp.	tarragon	15 mL
3	eggs, beaten	3
1 tsp.	sea salt	5 mL
1 cup	matzo meal	250 mL
	cooking oil	

Quick Béarnaise Sauce:

1 cup	mayonnaise	250 mL
¼ cup	tarragon vinegar	50 mL
2 tbsp.	minced fresh tarragon	25 mL
2 tbsp.	minced shallots	25 mL

Mix vegetables and tarragon. Then add eggs, salt, matzo meal and let mixture stand at room temperature for 30 minutes.

Form into patties and fry in shallow oil in skillet until golden brown on each side. Drain on absorbent towels and keep hot.

For sauce, mix together all ingredients and warm over low heat on the stove top. When just steaming, it is ready to be poured over cutlets to serve.

The potato has been misunderstood through the centuries! Although there have been devoted potato pushers in high places — Sir Walter Raleigh, Captain James Cook, Sir Francis Drake, persuading the "people" to accept the potato was difficult.

"Wareneki", a word of Russian origin is the Mennonite word for perogie, perogie being Ukranian.

At our house, wareneki were a meal. Mother, "boiled", while one of us sautéed, and another created the sauce. When the table was set and all seven of us were gathered, there would be 2 bowlfuls of wareneki, at least, which could easily be 3" by 4" (7 cm x 10 cm) in size! . . . and no one counted. . .

Wareneki or Perogies

Overall timing: 1 hour, 30 minutes   Serves: 6-8

1 cup	sour cream	250 mL
½ tsp.	salt	2 mL
2 cups	unbleached white flour	500 mL
1	egg white	1

Filling:

1½ cups	mashed potatoes (may be leftovers)	375 mL
½ cup	grated sharp Cheddar cheese	125 mL
1 tsp.	salt	5 mL
1	egg yolk	1
2 tbsp.	sweet cream	25 mL

Cream Gravy:

3 tbsp.	butter	45 mL
1 cup	sweet cream	250 mL

Mix sour cream, salt, flour, egg white into a smooth dough. Roll out fairly thin and cut into rounds with a large jar ring. Mix filling, beat well. Put 1 tbsp. (15 mL) filling on each round. Moisten edges of dough, turn 1 edge to make a half moon and pinch the edges. Make up the batch of wareneki, then get ready a large potful of boiling water. Drop wareneki into rapidly boiling water and boil for 5 minutes. Drain in a colander. Serve with sour cream, plain cream, or cream gravy. Wareneki may be sautéed until golden in butter after boiling. This makes them much tastier and not so "doughy".

For cream gravy, simply melt butter in a saucepan add cream and bring to a boil. Season if you wish.

Potato Gnocchi

Overall timing: 45 minutes   Serves: 6-8

8	**boiling, starchy (may be old) potatoes**	**8**
¾ cup	**unbleached white flour**	**175 mL**
2 tbsp.	**butter**	**25 mL**
2	**eggs**	**2**
1 tsp.	**salt**	**5 mL**

Pare and cook potatoes in a small amount of water. Drain, mash, and let cool. Add flour, butter, eggs, and salt. Hand mix from this point, adding flour until dough is not sticky. Knead until smooth. Boil a potful of salted water and drop gnocchi by the tablespoon (15 mL) into rapidly boiling water. Boil for 5 minutes. They will rise to the surface when they are ready to be removed. Drain in a colander. Heat a little butter in the frying pan and brown gnocchi, keep hot. Serve with Cream Gravy, page 82, sour cream, or Cheese and Tomato Sauce, page 84.

Acadian Potato Gnocchi Filling

Overall timing: 45 minutes   Serves: 8-10

2 cups	**ground pork**	**500 mL**
½ cup	**chopped dried apple**	**125 mL**
½ cup	**raisins**	**125 mL**
½ cup	**mashed potato (may be leftovers)**	**125 mL**
	salt and pepper	

Sauté pork with apple and raisins, drain away fat, reserving 2-3 tbsp. (25-45 mL) juices. Cool, then stir in mashed potato and more seasonings if desired. Place a rounded teaspoonful (5 mL) of this filling on a tablespoon (15 mL) of gnocchi mixture and fold over until filling is fully enclosed. Pinch to ensure a good seal and boil as directed above.

Cheese and Tomato Sauce

6	medium tomatoes, skinned, chopped	6
½ cup	water	125 mL
1 tsp.	sugar	5 mL
1 tsp.	basil flakes	5 mL
½ tsp.	salt	2 mL
⅛ tsp.	pepper	0.5 mL
¼ cup	grated Parmesan cheese	50 mL
½ cup	cottage cheese	125 mL

Gently boil skinned tomatoes in water with sugar and spices, 5-8 minutes. Add Parmesan cheese and cottage cheese. Pour into blender, and purée. Taste for seasonings. Return to saucepan and reheat. Serve hot.

Does anyone remember the special childhood occasions when riced potatoes were served?

Hot Riced Potatoes

Overall timing: 30 minutes   Serves: 6

5	large baking potatoes	5
2 tbsp.	butter	25 mL
1 tsp.	salt	5 mL
½ tsp.	white pepper	2 mL
1 tbsp.	chopped fresh parsley	15 mL

Pare and cook potatoes in a small amount of water until soft, about 20 minutes, with butter, salt, and pepper. Drain. When you are ready to serve, put potatoes through the ricer, do not stir. Serve on a pre-heated platter or bowl and sprinkle with parsley.

Antoine Auguste Parmentier, a French chemist and potato crusader, of the 18th Century, imprisoned in Germany in 1757, survived on only potatoes. Upon returning to France, he was somewhat shocked to find his countrymen still suspicious of the vegetable which had saved his life. With much good luck, Parmentier acquired a sandy piece of property, which no one wanted, from King Louis XVI — his ambition was to grow potatoes. Aware of the peasant mentality that "forbidden must be good", he asked the King to place guards about his field by day and withdraw them at night. The trick worked and night harvesting by local farmers began. Soon potatoes were blossoming all over France. France still remembers the "potato messiah" with gourmet dishes prepared, "à la Parmentier".

Thanks and salutations to Mr. Parmentier for his dedication to the potato cause, and for his good sense in promoting the potato.

Potato Parmentier

Overall timing: 40 minutes   Serves: 6

6	*medium baking potatoes*	6
2 cups	*milk*	500 mL
4 tbsp.	*butter*	60 mL
½ tsp.	*salt*	2 mL
½ tsp.	*freshly ground pepper*	2 mL
2	*onions, finely chopped*	2
2 tbsp.	*minced fresh parsley*	25 mL

Pare and boil potatoes until soft, in milk, half of butter, salt, and pepper. Meanwhile, sauté onion and parsley in remaining butter, until golden. Cover and simmer 5 minutes. Drain potatoes and rice, into a deep serving dish. Serve onion and parsley sauce over riced potatoes.

"All the way to Bailey's Bay, fish and taters every day!" Potatoes were first brought to Bermuda in 1612 by the English. They flourished exceedingly and soon became staples, alongside fish. It is interesting to note that the first cultivated potatoes in America came from Bermuda.

Bermuda Potatoes or Potatoes in Butter

Overall timing: 25 minutes   *Serves: 4-6*

½ lb.	butter	250 g
20-30	small, scrubbed, new potatoes	20-30
6	garlic cloves, chopped (optional)	6

Melt butter in a large oven casserole with a tight-fitting lid. Add potatoes and garlic, if using, cover and bake at 400°F (200°C) for 25 minutes. Serve with chopped mint and new lamb.

Provincial Potatoes

Overall timing: 30 minutes   *Serves: 6*

12-18	small new potatoes	12-18
¼ cup	butter	50 mL
3 tbsp.	olive oil	45 mL
	grated rind of ½ lemon	
⅛ tsp.	each grated nutmeg and pepper	0.5 mL
1 tsp.	flour	5 mL
½ tsp.	salt	2 mL
2 tbsp.	chopped fresh parsley	25 mL
1 tbsp.	chopped fresh chives	15 mL

Wash, then boil new potatoes in their skins. (You may use other boiling potatoes, but this recipe must be tried with new potatoes!) Into a saucepan put butter, oil, rind of lemon, nutmeg, pepper, flour, salt, parsley, chives and stir. Peel potatoes when cooked, cut if they are larger than walnut size, put into the butter sauce, heat, but do not let the butter boil. When ready to serve, add lemon juice. Serve hot.

New Potatoes/Peas/ Onions

Overall timing: 45 minutes   *Serves:* 6

12-18	small new potatoes, well-scrubbed	12-18
8	baby onions	8
1 cup	fresh garden peas	250 mL
1 tbsp.	butter	15 mL
¼ tsp.	marjoram	1 mL

Boil new potatoes in a small amount of water until tender. Boil onions and peas together in a small amount of water until tender, 5-8 minutes. Drain vegetables, reserving water, stir together with butter and marjoram.

Call it pomatoes or topatoes.

New Potatoes and Tomatoes

Overall timing: 40 minutes   *Serves:* 6

2 tbsp.	butter	25 mL
12	small white onions	12
2 tbsp.	flour	25 mL
5	medium new potatoes, scrubbed, sliced	5
2	cloves garlic, crushed	2
1 tsp.	thyme	5 mL
1	bay leaf	1
1 tsp.	salt	5 mL
½ tsp.	freshly ground pepper	2 mL
4	large tomatoes, peeled, chopped	4

Melt butter in a 3-quart (3 L) saucepan and brown onions. Then sprinkle onions with flour and mix well. Add potatoes, garlic, thyme, bay leaf, salt, and pepper to cooked onions and cover with water. Simmer gently for 25 minutes. For the last 5 minutes add chopped, skinned tomatoes and cook until tomatoes are tender. Drain. Reserve water for use in soups or stews.

This is a trusty recipe for "older" potatoes.

Diced Potatoes with Sour Cream

Overall timing: 30 minutes   Serves: 4-6

4	large boiling potatoes, peeled, diced	4
2 tbsp.	butter	25 mL
1	onion, chopped	1
1 tbsp.	chopped parsley	15 mL
1 cup	sour cream	250 mL
1 tsp.	Worcestershire sauce	5 mL

Prepare potatoes, boil and drain. Place in a serving dish. In saucepan melt butter and sauté onion in it. Add parsley and sour cream, heat, do not boil. Stir in Worcestershire sauce, and pour over potatoes, mixing well. Good with farmer sausage.

For the pepper and garlic fan

Pepperoni Con Patate

Overall timing: 40 minutes   Serves: 4-6

4	cloves garlic, crushed	4
2 tbsp.	olive oil	25 mL
4	sweet green peppers, cut into strips	4
1	onion, minced	1
4	boiling potatoes, peeled, sliced	4
1 tsp.	salt	5 mL
½ tsp.	freshly ground pepper	2 mL
1 cup	tomato juice	250 mL

In a 3-quart (3 L) saucepan, sauté garlic in olive oil. Add other ingredients, boil, covered, for 30 minutes, stirring occasionally. Adding more tomato juice if needed.

Romanoff Potatoes

Overall timing: 1 hour, 20 minutes   Serves: 6

6	*large boiling potatoes*	*6*
1 cup	*sharp grated Cheddar cheese*	*250 mL*
2 cups	*sour cream*	*500 mL*
2 tbsp.	*chopped green onions*	*25 mL*
2 tbsp.	*chopped fresh parsley*	*25 mL*
1 tsp.	*paprika*	*5 mL*

Boil potatoes in their jackets until tender. Cool. Peel and grate them into a bowl and combine with ½ of the Cheddar cheese and all of the sour cream, onions, and parsley. Put into a 3-4-cup (1 L) casserole, sprinkle with the additional cheese and paprika. Bake at 350°F (180°C), uncovered, for 30-40 minutes. Serve immediately.

Potato and Carrot Mold

Overall timing: 1 hour   Serves: 6

4	*large boiling potatoes*	*4*
3	*large carrots*	*3*
2 cups	*milk*	*500 mL*
1 tbsp.	*butter*	*15 mL*
1 tsp.	*salt*	*5 mL*
¼ tsp.	*white pepper*	*1 mL*
1 tsp.	*lemon juice*	*5 mL*
¼ tsp.	*ground ginger*	*1 mL*

Peel potatoes and carrots, boil together in salted water, until tender. Mash. Add milk, butter, salt, pepper, lemon juice and ginger. Beat until smooth and fluffy, pour into a buttered 2-quart (2 L) casserole, and bake at 350°F (180°C), until browned. Serve with a cheese sauce.

Cheese Sauce:

2 cups	*shredded old Cheddar cheese*	*500 mL*
⅓ cup	*milk*	*75 mL*

Melt cheese over hot water. Slowly stir in milk.

South American potato stock revived the Irish stock after the great blight of 1845. Within a week, "late blight" fungus can destroy a potato plant. In that summer of 1845, rainy cool weather was the needed factor to spread the "late blight", which incidently is still the worst plague of potatoes today, and it resulted in six frightful years of famine, leading to a million deaths in Ireland. Many more died at sea on their way to America. The potato has been vital in man's survival! The lack of King Potato has resulted in starvation.

Stoved Irish Potatoes

Overall timing: 35 minutes   Serves: 6

8	*medium boiling potatoes, sliced*	8
3	*onions, thinly sliced*	3
1 tsp.	*salt*	5 mL
½ tsp.	*white pepper*	2 mL
½ cup	*chopped parsley*	125 mL
¼ cup	*bacon or chicken fat*	50 mL
1½ cups	*beef stock*	375 mL

Arrange potatoes and onions in a a heavy skillet. Season each layer with salt, pepper, and parsley. Dot with fat. Add beef stock, cover and simmer for 25 minutes or until liquid is partially absorbed.
*You may use butter instead of bacon or chicken fat.

Potatoes with Sorrel

Overall timing: 1 hour   Serves: 4

3 tbsp.	*butter*	45 mL
3	*medium boiling potatoes, sliced thin*	3
2 cups	*chopped sorrel*	500 mL
2 tsp.	*ground chervil*	10 mL
2	*cloves garlic, minced*	2
1 cup	*hot beef stock*	250 mL
	butter	

Melt butter in a 2-quart (2 L) casserole, add a layer of potatoes, season. Add sorrel, mixed with chervil and garlic. Add another layer of potatoes, season. Add beef stock, tiny dabs of butter and bake at 400°F (200°C) for 45 minutes, until cooked and tender.

Dutch Potato-Broccoli

Overall timing: 1 hour   Serves: 4-6

3	large boiling potatoes, pared, diced	3
1½ cups	cream	375 mL
½ cup	water	125 mL
1 tbsp.	cornstarch	15 mL
2 cups	chopped fresh broccoli	500 mL
½ cup	smooth peanut butter	125 mL
1	onion, sliced	1
	Parmesan cheese	

Cook potatoes in cream and water until done. Do not drain, thicken with cornstarch mixed with a small amount of water. Meanwhile, chop broccoli into 1-2" (2.5-5 cm) chunks and cook until fork tender. Add to potato mixture, along with peanut butter and onion. Stir well to mix. Put into a buttered 3-quart (3 L) casserole and sprinkle generously with Parmesan cheese. Bake at 350°F (180°C) for 30 minutes.

Danish Caramel Potatoes

Overall timing: 30 minutes   Serves: 4

12	small (walnut-size) new potatoes	12
½ cup	sugar	125 mL
½ cup	melted butter	125 mL

Boil unpeeled new potatoes for 15 minutes, do not overboil. Cool slightly, then peel. Melt the sugar in a heavy skillet over very low heat. Cook slowly for 3-5 minutes until sugar turns a light caramel color. Stir constantly with a spoon, the syrup changes color very rapidly and burns easily. It must not become too dark or it will be bitter. Stir in melted butter, add as many potatoes as possible without crowding. Constantly shake the pan to coat them on all sides with the caramel. Remove the caramelized potatoes to a heated serving bowl, repeat procedure until all potatoes are coated. Serve hot.

In Denmark, Caramel Potatoes are a Christmas specialty, but they can be enjoyed at any time of year. They are nice served with chicken or roast duck.

This Indian version of boiled potatoes is unique in flavor and appeal. As coconut milk is hard to find in this country, you can make your own, by draining a coconut and making milk from the water, or you may substitute water and 2 tbsp. (25 mL) finely chopped coconut.

Vegetable Curry

Overall timing: 40 minutes   Serves: 4

5	medium boiling potatoes, peeled, sliced	5
⅛ tsp.	ground saffron	0.5 mL
2 tbsp.	curry powder	25 mL
1 tsp.	salt	5 mL
1 tbsp.	dill seeds	15 mL
1	bay leaf	1
½"	piece red chili	1.3 cm
1	clove garlic, sliced	1
½	chopped onion	½
2 cups	coconut milk	500 mL

Prepare potatoes. Then blend with all seasonings and onion and add 1½ cups (375 mL) of the coconut milk. Simmer until sauce boils down, about 25 minutes. Add another ½ cup (125 mL) coconut milk, reheat. Serve with lamb kabobs.

*Note, saffron, which is expensive, adds bright color, but little flavor. Remember to use it sparingly. Turmeric may be used as an inexpensive substitute.

Growing peas and beans and other above-ground crops, often led to failure in pioneer times, especially on the North American Prairies, where droughts and dust storms ravaged. When all else failed, the versatile, below-the-ground potato survived. Potatoes provided an abundantly nutritious food for homesteaders in this country. They often provided the ONLY, much-needed, source of Vitamin C. One potato contains half the recommended daily supply of Vitamin C, approximately 23 mg.

Steamed Potatoes

Steam enough potatoes just to cover the bottom of the steamer. For larger quantities boiling is a better idea. Steaming is the best way to retain the actual texture and nutrients of the potato. New potatoes do not need to be peeled, but older and "tougher-skinned" potatoes should be peeled. Bring water to a boil in steamer and place potatoes in the basket. Cover and steam for 13-15 minutes. Old potatoes will take slightly longer to cook, while slices of potato will be faster. Serve with chopped fresh herbs such as chives or parsley and season to taste!

Mashed Potatoes

Overall timing: 30 minutes   Serves: 6

6	large boiling potatoes	6
½-1 cup	milk (depends on type of potato used)	125-250 mL
2 tbsp.	butter OR 1 tsp. (5 mL) chicken soup powder	15 mL
½ tsp.	salt	2 mL
½ tsp.	freshly ground pepper	2 mL
sprinkle	ground nutmeg (optional)	sprinkle

Use a large saucepan to cook potatoes, which have been pared and either left whole or cut into chunks. Add a SMALL amount of water. Cover and boil gently until fork tender, 15-20 minutes. Drain, RE-SERVING WATER, for gravy, soup stock, or bread. I find that mashing potatoes by hand results in a fluffy mashed potato, whereas beating with a hand mixer tends to make then "gluey" and sticky. Again, it depends on type of potato used, how dry or wet it is, and your personal preference. Mash until no lumps remain and add desired amount of milk, "less is always best" is a good rule to abide by. Stir in butter, salt, and pepper, (substitute soup stock for butter to reduce calories).

NOTE: For wee babes, omit salt, pepper, and soup stock.

Creamed Potatoes

Beat boiled potatoes with a mixer or blender. Use the same method and ingredients as for mashed potatoes, but to avoid "gluey" potatoes, you should use a dry potato. Simply beat until all lumps are gone.

From Pennsylvania, U.S.A., a Berks county potato recipe which you serve as a vegetable. In Pennsylvania, it could appear with Scrapple, a pork and cornmeal dish, or a Veal and Tripe Stew!

Berks County Potato Dish

Overall timing: 1 hour, 30 minutes   Serves: 8

1½ cups	mashed potatoes (may be leftovers)	375 mL
2	eggs, beaten	2
1 cup	light cream	250 mL
5	slices of white bread	5
1	onion, diced	1
2 tbsp.	butter	25 mL
	salt and pepper to taste	

Thoroughly blend mashed potatoes and eggs with a beater. Add cream and set aside. Cut bread into ½" (1.3 cm) cubes and brown with onion in butter. Stir onions and bread into potato mixture and add seasonings. Turn into a greased casserole and bake in a preheated moderate oven 375°F (190°C) for 1 hour. Serve hot with main course.

Potato Frosted Eggplant

Overall timing: 40 minutes   Serves: 4-6

1	medium onion, chopped	1
¼ cup	chicken stock	50 mL
2 cups	fresh tomatoes, skinned, chopped	500 mL
⅛ tsp.	crushed chilies	0.5 mL
2	cloves garlic, minced	2
1	large eggplant, pared, cubed, cooked (5 min.)	1
2	eggs, well beaten	2
1 cup	mashed potatoes (may be leftovers)	250 mL
2 tbsp.	Parmesan cheese	25 mL

Stew onion, in chicken stock with tomatoes, chilies, and garlic for 5 minutes. Add drained cooked eggplant, eggs. Pour into a greased 2-quart (2 L) casserole, top with mashed potatoes and Parmesan cheese. Bake at 350°F (180°C) for 30 minutes.

Mashed Potatoes with Cream Cheese

Overall timing: 40 minutes   Serves: 4-6

6	medium boiling potatoes	6
3 oz.	cream cheese, softened	85 g
3 tbsp.	butter	45 mL
1 tsp.	salt	5 mL
¼-½ cup	milk	50-125 mL
2 tbsp.	chives	25 mL

Peel the potatoes and boil in salted water until tender. Drain. Add softened cream cheese, butter, salt. Beat with an electric mixer until light, fluffy, and smooth. Add enough milk to make potatoes a creamy consistency, but not too much so that they are wet! Stir in chives and place in a serving dish.

Julia Child's Mashed Potatoes with Garlic

Overall timing: 30 minutes   Serves: 4-6

6	large boiling potatoes, pared, chunked	6
1	head garlic, peeled	1
3 tbsp.	butter	45 mL
1 tbsp.	flour	15 mL
½ cup	cream	125 mL
1 tsp.	salt	5 mL
½ tsp.	freshly ground pepper	2 mL
1 tbsp.	butter	15 mL

Boil potatoes, drain, and rice. Make sauce by simmering 1 whole head of garlic cloves in a covered saucepan with butter, about 20 minutes. Beat in flour, whisk in cream and seasonings. Bring to a boil, cook for 1 minute, and purée. Add this purée to riced potatoes and heat together to evaporate moisture. Add extra butter!

Dutchess Potatoes

Overall timing: 45 minutes   Serves: 4-6

6	large boiling potatoes, pared, cooked, mashed (keep hot)	6
3	egg yolks, beaten	3
3 tbsp.	melted butter	45 mL
1 tsp.	salt	5 mL
½ tsp.	freshly ground pepper	2 mL
1	egg white, beaten with 1 tbsp. (15 mL) water	1

Add next 4 ingredients to mashed potatoes. Cool slightly. Put mashed potatoes into a forcing bag fitted with a large fluted nozzle rosette tube. Pipe into individual rosettes. Mound the rosette to approximately 2" (5 cm) high by 1½-2" (4-5 cm) wide, as you pipe it onto a greased baking sheet. Make 12 for 4 people, 3 look best on a plate. Glaze with beaten egg white and bake at 425°F (220°C) until golden brown, 8-10 minutes. Arrange around a roast of meat or place on individual plates.

Potatoes Paprika

Overall timing: 30 minutes   Serves: 4-6

2	onions, chopped	2
1 tbsp.	bacon fat	15 mL
4	boiling potatoes, scrubbed, sliced	4
4 tsp.	paprika	20 mL
1 tsp.	seasoned salt	5 mL
¼ tsp.	sherry pepper sauce	1 mL
½ cup	potato water	125 mL

Brown onions in fat, add potatoes and paprika. Cover and cook over moderate heat for 10 minutes, stirring occasionally. Reduce heat, add salt, sherry peppers sauce, and water. Cook, covered, for another 10 minutes.

Sesame Potato Logs

Overall timing: 3 hours   Serves: 4

¼ cup	milk	50 mL
2	eggs divided, see directions	2
2 tbsp.	butter	25 mL
½ tsp.	salt	2 mL
3 cups	warm mashed potatoes	750 mL
1 cup	flour	250 mL
2-3 oz.	sesame seeds	55-85 g

Add milk, 1 egg, butter and salt to mashed potatoes, beat with mixer until smooth. Spread out in a 8" x 12" (20 cm x 30 cm) pan and chill, covered. Prepare 2 shallow bowls, 1 with beaten egg plus 2 tbsp. (25 mL) water, 1 with a cup (250 mL) of flour, and a large plate with sesame seeds. Cut cooled mashed potatoes into 2" x 1" (5 cm x 2.5 cm) pieces, roll in flour, lift into egg mix, turn them over. Set logs in sesame seeds roll over, covering with seeds. Put into buttered 13" x 9" (33 cm x 23 cm) baking dish, and bake 15-20 minutes at 450°F (230°C) until golden brown.

Potato Croquettes

Overall timing: 45 minutes   Serves: 6-8

2 cups	cold mashed potatoes (may be leftovers)	500 mL
4 cups	minced raw spinach	1 L
2 tbsp.	butter	25 mL
2	eggs	2
1 tbsp.	curry powder (optional)	15 mL
1 tsp.	salt	5 mL
½ tsp.	freshly ground pepper	2 mL
1	egg, beaten with 1 tbsp. (15 mL) water	1
2 cups	fine bread crumbs	500 mL
½ cup	grated Parmesan cheese	125 mL

Cook spinach and add to cold mashed potatoes along with butter, eggs, curry powder, salt, and pepper. Mix well. Shape into croquettes, about 1½" (4 cm) balls. Dip into egg mixture and roll in combined bread crumbs and Parmesan cheese. Fry in fat in a deep fryer at 380°F (190°C) 1-2 minutes, until golden brown. May be refrigerated and warmed at 400°F (200°C) for 12-15 minutes or served immediately.

Potatoes add a softness to turnips when mashed and served together, truly delicious!

Potatoes and Turnips

Overall timing: 40 minutes   *Serves: 6*

3 cups	**turnip, peeled, diced**	**750 mL**
6	**large boiling potatoes, peeled, diced**	**6**
1 tsp.	**onion salt**	**5 mL**
½ tsp.	**white pepper**	**2 mL**
1 tsp.	**paprika**	**5 mL**
1 tbsp.	**chicken stock powder**	**15 mL**
1 tsp.	**horseradish**	**5 mL**
1 tsp.	**brown sugar**	**5 mL**

Cook turnips for 5 minutes. Add potatoes, onion salt, bring to a boil and continue cooking until tender, about 20 minutes. Drain if necessary. Mash vegetables together with other ingredients, serve hot.

This stuffing is especially nice with wild fowl.

Potato Stuffing

Overall timing: 20 minutes   *Serves: 6-8*

For 3 lb. (1.5 kg) Duck:

6	**large potatoes, boiled, mashed**	**6**
1 cup	**diced celery**	**250 mL**
1 tbsp.	**chopped onion**	**15 mL**
	cut-up duck giblets	
2 tbsp.	**butter**	**25 mL**
½ cup	**milk**	**125 mL**
1 tsp.	**salt**	**5 mL**
½ tsp.	**pepper**	**2 mL**
2 tbsp.	**minced fresh parsley**	**25 mL**

Prepare mashed potatoes. Sauté celery, onion, and chopped giblets in butter until browned. Add milk, cover and simmer for 5 minutes. Mix together mashed potatoes and giblet mixture, salt, pepper and parsley. Fill duck quite firmly with stuffing.

Does suspicion still hang over the potato? Nutritionists are recommending a diet which includes potatoes at least once a day. Canada's Food Guide shows a picture of the potato along with the tomato, carrot, and radish! The vegetable that provided food surplus for the population expansion necessary to our country's industrial growth, now contributes to a long lifetime for man.

Potato Dumplings

Overall timing: 45 minutes   Serves: 4-6

2 cups	hot mashed potatoes	500 mL
3	eggs, beaten	3
1 tbsp.	grated onion	15 mL
1 cup	fine bread crumbs	250 mL
½ cup	unbleached flour	125 mL
1 tsp.	baking powder	5 mL
1 tbsp.	chopped parsley	15 mL

Pare, chunk and boil 3-4 boiling type potatoes. Drain and mash. Combine potatoes and other ingredients. Mix well and drop by tablespoonfuls (15 mL) into hot stew, gravy, or consommé. Cover and cook 20-25 minutes.

Serve plain or with sauce, well buttered or herbed.

Potato Noodles

Overall timing: 1 hour   Serves: 6

6	large potatoes, pared, chunked	6
2 tsp.	salt	10 mL
4 tbsp.	flour, white or whole-wheat	60 mL
3	eggs	3
2 tbsp.	butter	25 mL

Boil potatoes in a small amount of water, drain. Mash potatoes, then add salt, flour, and eggs. Knead into a dough and roll out on lightly floured board. Cut into strips about ¼" x 4" (1 cm x 10 cm). Place in buttered baking dish, in a crisscross arrangement. Dot with butter and bake in moderate oven, 375°F (190°C) until nicely browned, about 30 minutes. Good with Stroganoff or Schnitzel.

"Give yourself plenty of time for these to cook. I seem to get fooled at times with Scalloped Potatoes, as baking time varies with potato varieties."

Scalloped Potatoes

Overall timing: 1 hour, 30 minutes   *Serves: 4-6*

3 tbsp.	*butter*	*45 mL*
2 tbsp.	*unbleached white flour*	*25 mL*
3 cups	*milk*	*750 mL*
1 tsp.	*salt*	*5 mL*
¼ tsp.	*freshly ground pepper*	*1 mL*
6	*medium boiling potatoes, pared, thinly sliced*	*6*
1	*onion, chopped*	*1*

Make white sauce of first 5 ingredients. Melt butter in a saucepot over high heat. Stir in flour, blend, then gradually add milk, stirring constantly. Season with salt and pepper. Put half the potatoes in a greased 2-quart (2 L) casserole. Cover with half the onion and half the sauce. Repeat layers.

Cover and bake at 350°F (180°C) about 1 hour. Uncover and continue baking until top is nicely browned.

Variations:

To sauce add:
— 1½ tbsp. (25 mL) horseradish and 1-2 tsp. (5-10 mL) prepared mustard, Dijon style.
— ½ cup (125 mL) sliced fresh mushrooms and ½ cup (125 mL) grated Parmesan cheese.
— 1 cup (250 mL) grated sharp Cheddar cheese and ¼ cup (50 mL) chopped green onion.
— 3 cloves crushed garlic
— ½ cup (125 mL) chopped green pepper
— 3 tbsp. (45 mL) beef stock mixed into the milk.

Home-Fried Potatoes

Overall timing: 30 minutes   Serves: 6

4-6	boiling potatoes, washed, with or without skins on	4-6
1-2 tbsp.	butter or bacon fat	15-25 mL
1 tsp.	salt	5 mL
½ tsp.	freshly ground pepper	2 mL
1-2 tsp.	chopped mixed herbs — rosemary, summer savoury, basil, chives, marjoram, parsley, mint, oregano	5-10 mL

Slice potatoes about ¼" (1 cm) thick, or to taste. Melt and heat fat in a skillet and add sliced potatoes. Fry over moderate heat until golden brown and fork tender. Then to the end of cooking time add seasonings.

Variations:
— Add ½ cup (125 mL) chopped onions or 1 tsp. (5 mL) onion powder.
— Add 2 cloves garlic, crushed.
— Add ½ cup (125 mL) finely chopped sweet peppers.
— Add 1 tsp. (5 mL) chili powder.
— Add ½-1 cup (125-250 mL) cracklings or crumbled bacon.
— Add ½ cup (125 mL) grated Parmesan cheese.

Baked or Boiled Potatoes, Home-Fried

Overall timing: 15 minutes   Serves: 4

4	leftover cooked potatoes	4
1-2 tbsp.	butter or bacon fat	15-25 mL
	dash salt and pepper	

Slice potatoes, melt fat in frying pan and sauté potatoes until nicely browned, turning and stirring often. Season to taste.

101

This recipe comes from a restaurant in France, the Auvergnat.

Potato Cheese Truffade

Overall timing: 50 minutes   Serves: 6-8

8	medium, boiling, waxy potatoes	8
⅓ lb.	slab bacon	170 g
1 tsp.	salt	5 mL
½ tsp.	freshly ground pepper	2 mL
2 cups	*Tomme de Savoy cheese, diced (specialty shop)	500 mL
2 tbsp.	freshly chopped parsley	25 mL
2 tbsp.	oil	25 mL

Slice, the potatoes, peeled, into ⅛" (3 mm) rounds, dropping them into a bowl of cold water as they are sliced. In a large saucepan, sauté bacon, diced, until it is lightly browned. Drain the potatoes and pat them dry with paper towels. Add them to the pan, sprinkle with salt and pepper and toss the potatoes over high heat until they are coated with fat, cook the potatoes covered, over moderately low heat, tossing them occasionally, for 25 minutes. Remove pan from heat and add cheese and parsley. In a large heavy skillet heat oil, spoon in the potato mixture, tamping it down evenly, and brown it over medium heat. Turn truffade out, browned side up, on a heated platter.

*Substitute — Camembert cheese

Savory Saxon Dumpling

Overall timing: 1 hour, 30 minutes   Serves: 8-10

8	medium baking potatoes, raw	8
1 cup	buttermilk	250 mL
4	medium potatoes, boiled, cooled	4
1 tsp.	salt	5 mL
1 tsp.	nutmeg	5 mL
½-1 cup	flour	125-250 mL

Grate raw potatoes, squeeze out the moisture. Put in a wide bowl, add buttermilk, and grate in boiled potatoes. Mix well, add seasonings. Spoon off dumplings by the tablespoonful (15 mL). Using floured hands, fashion them into balls, roll in flour. Fry in ½" (1.3 cm) hot fat in a heavy skillet. Eat with roast pork, red cabbage, and sauerkraut.

Hearty, chewy and filling, Norwegian Potato Lefser, epitomize the Christmas spirit there and are altogether satisfying. They are served as a bread.

Updated Potato Lefser

Overall timing: 4 hours   Serves: 8

8	medium potatoes, peeled, boiled	8
¼ cup	butter	50 mL
3-4 tbsp.	rich cream	45-60 mL
2 tsp.	salt	10 mL
¼ tsp.	freshly ground pepper	1 mL
2 cups	white bleached flour	500 mL

Mash potatoes, then measure a full 4 cups (1 L) and return to a bowl. Add butter, cream, salt, pepper, beat well and chill for 2 hours. Then add 1 cup (250 mL) of flour to potato mixture to form a smooth dough. Sprinkle more flour on a pastry cloth, form ¼ cup (50 mL) of dough into a ball and flatten it slightly on the cloth. Sprinkle top with more flour and roll dough out to an 8" (20 cm) round. (If dough does not stick together, gather it into a ball, add another tbsp. (15 mL) of flour to cloth and reroll dough.) To cook, heat an ungreased cast iron frying pan or grill until it is moderately hot. Transfer lefser very carefully to grill, then prick several times. Cook for a total of 3-4 minutes, turning often, until the lefser is lightly browned and dry on both sides, but still tender.

Cook remaining lefser in similar manner, keep warm. To serve, halve or cut into 4 wedges, spread with butter and roll up.

Variation:

— Add ¼ cup (50 mL) sugar to mixture or ⅛ cup (25 mL) grated Parmesan cheese. Serve with mashed potatoes and Nutmeg Meatballs in Gravy.

This is an interesting accompaniment for meat dishes.

Israeli Potato Maraska

Overall timing: 30 minutes   *Serves: 6*

6	boiling potatoes, peeled, cooked, mashed, warm	6
2	eggs	2
2 tbsp.	cream	25 mL
2 tbsp.	chopped fresh parsley	25 mL
2	minced onions	2
2 tsp.	seasoned salt	10 mL
¼ cup	minced cooked ham or fish (optional)	50 mL

Mix all ingredients together, fashion balls the size of cherries. Place on a buttered baking sheet and bake at 425°F (220°C) for 15-20 minutes, until nicely browned. Serve with main course. May be made up to 2 days ahead and kept refrigerated.

Gruyère Cheese Potatoes

Overall timing: 1 hour, 15 minutes   *Serves 4-6*

	butter	
1	clove garlic, minced	1
3 cups	sliced peeled, boiling potatoes	750 mL
1½ cups	boiling milk	375 mL
1	egg, beaten	1
½ tsp.	salt	2 mL
⅛ tsp.	freshly grated pepper	0.5 mL
⅛ tsp.	nutmeg	0.5 mL
1 cup	grated Gruyère cheese	250 mL
	butter	

Generously butter a 3-quart (3 L) baking dish and rub with the minced garlic, discard garlic. Place potatoes in dish. Mix beaten egg into the hot milk, season with salt, pepper, nutmeg, and add ¾ cup (175 mL) of the grated Gruyère cheese. Mix gently and pour over potatoes. Sprinkle with other ¼ cup (50 mL) of grated cheese and dot with butter. Bake at 375°F (190°C) for 1 hour or until tender.

A most beautiful potato dish! It requires boiling type potatoes, that should be starchy enough to hold together and form a cake.
(Starch test for potatoes on page 41.)

Petal Potatoes or Potatoes Anna

Overall timing: 1 hour   Serves: 8

9	**medium, starchy boiling potatoes, pared, sliced, sliced ¼" (1 cm) thick**	9
6 tbsp.	**melted butter**	90 mL
2 tbsp.	**chopped parsley**	25 mL
½ tsp.	**freshly ground pepper**	2 mL

Pat dry potato petals. Heat oven to 425°F (220°C). Pour half of the butter into a glass 9" (23 cm) pie plate. Place dish over low heat and when butter is hot begin layering potato petals in circles, beginning in center of pan. Lightly drizzle each layer with butter, parsley, and pepper. Top potatoes with tin foil, seal edges. Press potatoes down with a saucepan to pack tightly. Bake in oven for 25 minutes, then press down again. Bake for another 25 minutes without tin foil. Potato petals are done when tender and edges are nicely browned. Pour off excess butter and shake pan to make sure potatoes are loose. Invert on a preheated platter to serve.

Party Potato Nests

Overall timing: 2 hours   *Serves: 12*

The potato nests are created with special long-handled nested wire baskets that are available in cookware stores. Nests are crisper if fried twice. The first frying can be done up to 2 days ahead.

Potato Nests

3½ lbs.	*dry potatoes, peeled*	*2 kg*
	vegetable oil (for deep-frying)	

Shred potatoes into ⅛" (3 mm) thick julienne strips, and soak for 15 minutes in a bowl of salted cold water. Pour oil into deep-fryer to depth of 3" (8 cm) and heat to 375°F (190°C). Drain potatoes and dry thoroughly. Line 4½" (11 cm) potato nest basket fryer with 1 cup (250 mL) of potatoes. Clamp smaller basket on top. Lower fryer into oil; oil will bubble up. Lift fryer up and down until bubbles subside, about 1 minute. Fry until nests are light brown. Slip off clamps and twist basket to separate. Hold potato nest with a paper towel and slowly twist to release. Drain nest. Repeat with remaining potato, reheating oil to 375°F (190°C) before each batch. These can be made 2 days ahead and stored in an airtight container.

Stir-Fried Beef and Vegetables

Overall timing: 1 hour, 30 minutes   Serves: 12

1 lb.	sirloin steak, cut into ⅛" (3 mm) strips	500 g
2	medium green bell peppers, cut into ⅛" (3 mm) strips	2
2	medium red bell peppers, cut into ⅛" (3 mm) strips	2
2	medium yellow bell peppers, cut into ⅛" (3 mm) strips	2
12 oz.	bamboo shoots	340 g
1	large onion, cut into ⅛" (3 mm) strips	1
4	slices peeled fresh ginger, quarter-size, minced	4
4	large cloves, minced	4

Sauce:

2 tbsp.	soy sauce	25 mL
2 tbsp.	dry sherry	25 mL
4 tsp.	red wine vinegar	20 mL
2 tbsp.	sesame seeds	25 mL
2 tsp.	chili paste with garlic (available at oriental markets)	10 mL
1 tsp.	sugar	5 mL
½ tsp.	coarsely ground peppercorns	2 mL
2 tsp.	cornstarch (dissolved in 5 tsp. (25 mL) water	10 mL

Heat wok, add a few tsp. (mL) oil. Stir-fry beef for 2-3 minutes, push up sides; add vegetables and cook only until vegetables are light brown and still crispy. Mix sauce, pour into wok, toss with meat and vegetables until coated with sauce. Spoon into bowl and serve immediately in Potato Nests, page 106.

Rösti

Overall timing: 1 hour   Serves: 4

4	large boiling potatoes	4
½ cup	minced shallots or green onions	125 mL
½ tsp.	salt	2 mL
¼ tsp.	freshly grated pepper	1 mL
4 tbsp.	butter	60 mL

Peel potatoes and boil in a small amount of water until tender. Drain and chill well. Grate coarsely and, in a bowl, combine them with shallots, salt, and pepper. In a heavy skillet heat 2 tbsp. (25 mL) of the butter, add potato mixture and flatten down in skillet to form a cake. Cook cake for 12 minutes, until bottom is brown and crusty. Loosen edge of cake and slide it onto a plate. Invert cake onto another plate. In skillet heat other 2 tbsp. (25 mL) butter and slide cake, uncooked side down, into skillet and cook for another 10 minutes or so to brown. Remove from heat, carefully slide potato cake onto a heated platter to serve.

Bechamel Potatoes

Overall timing: 1 hour   Serves: 6

6	large baking potatoes	6
3 tbsp.	butter	45 mL
1-2 tbsp.	flour	15-25 mL
¾ cup	water	175 mL
1 cup	sour cream	250 mL
1 tsp.	salt	5 mL
½ tsp.	paprika	2 mL
½ tsp.	nutmeg	2 mL
1 tsp.	beef extract	5 mL
2 tbsp.	chopped chives	25 mL
1 tsp.	lemon rind	5 mL
1 tsp.	chopped fresh dill	5 mL

Wash potatoes, bake in their jackets until tender. Peel. Melt butter in a saucepan, stir in flour. Slowly add enough water to form a creamy sauce, beating with a whisk. Add sour cream, salt, paprika, nutmeg, beef extract, chives, lemon rind, and dill. Slice the still-warm potatoes into the hot sauce. Serve with ham, sausage, or hard-boiled eggs.

Mixed Baked Vegetables

Overall timing: 1 hour   *Serves: 4-6*

1 tbsp.	*butter*	*15 mL*
4	*medium baking potatoes, pared*	*4*
3	*green peppers*	*3*
3	*tomatoes*	*3*
4	*onions*	*4*
1 cup	*zucchini squash*	*250 mL*
¼ cup	*hot chicken broth*	*50 mL*
1 tsp.	*freshly ground pepper*	*5 mL*

Preheat oven to 400°F (200°C). Butter a medium-size baking dish. Quarter vegetables. Approximate size of chunks should be 1" x 2" (2.5 cm x 5 cm), keep uniform in size. Put into baking dish, pour chicken broth over and sprinkle with pepper. Cover and bake for 45 minutes.

Garlic Potatoes with Cumin Seed

Overall timing: 45 minutes   *Serves: 4*

4	*medium baking potatoes*	*4*
1-2 tbsp.	*butter*	*15-25 mL*
6	*cloves garlic, sliced thinly*	*6*
1 tbsp.	*cumin seed*	*15 mL*

Scrub potatoes well. Halve potatoes. Heat oven to 425°F (220°C). Cut a cross on each potato half and fill with a good dab of butter and slices of garlic, sprinkle with cumin seed. Bake for 30 minutes on a cookie sheet or on oven rack. Butter may drip a little so place a tin foil plate under potatoes to prevent the fat from descending on the oven element. For Barbecue: To cook on barbecue, proceed as for oven baking or wrap in tin foil and bake on the hot grill for 25 minutes, turning once.

Roasting Potatoes

For roasted potatoes, simply prepare small peeled potatoes or peel and chunk the larger ones. I prefer roasting baking potatoes, because drier potatoes soak up more flavor and juices from the pan. But, they also absorb some of the fat, so this is a consideration.

I roast potatoes alongside many types of meat, beef, lamb, chicken, pork and moose. You also save time and electrical energy by roasting potatoes along with meat, the same applies to baking potatoes.

Roast Caraway Potatoes

Overall timing: 45 minutes   Serves: 4-6

12	*small baking potatoes, pared*	*12*
	roast of meat	
1-2 tsp.	*caraway seeds (optional)*	*5-10 mL*

Prepare potatoes and place in roasting pan, around the roast of meat. Sprinkle with caraway seeds (optional). Potatoes will take 30-40 minutes to cook at 350°F (180°C) — less time if roasted at a higher temperature, but more time if roaster is crowded. Time the roast so that the potatoes and meat are done at the same time. Remove roast from pan, leave potatoes in pan and put under broiler until puffed and dark golden brown, basting with pan juices.

Variations:
— For flavor try adding small whole onions or other herbs such as dill, tarragon, and various spices.

BAKED STUFFED POTATOES

The elite baking potatoes are Idaho Russets and Netted Gems. They are perhaps the most famous baking potatoes of all and justifiably so. When baked, without tin foil, they are mealy and fluffy inside and have a crispy, chewy exterior. The only time I wrap them in tin foil is when we are camping and then they are baked directly on the coals.

Other potatoes can be baked the same way as Idaho Russets and Netted Gems, but the textures differ.

Baking Potatoes

Scrub potatoes well. Pat dry. Skins may be rubbed with oil for a less crisp exterior. Bake in a preheated oven at 450°F (230°C) or 400°F (200°C) until tender, to 40-50 minutes. Cooking time will depend on potato size. Pierce only to test for doneness. When cooked, cut into the top of potato and squeeze the bottom to push up and plump the flesh. Eat as they are or with butter and/or a choice of garnishes.

*To make potato portions smaller, for instance if you are serving stuffed potatoes with a substantial dinner, cut baked potatoes in half, before scooping out the center, and stuff the halves with any of the following fillings.

Microwave Potatoes

Baking 4 potatoes at a time, on high, should take approximately 15-18 minutes. More time will be needed if you bake more potatoes all at once. Also when baked in the microwave they have a tendency to split if not pierced.

 The Irish still believe that a day without potatoes is a day without nourishment. The potato "garden" in Ireland is held in esteem. The very names of Irish potatoes are blithesome poetry, not to mention gastronomic visions: Golden Wonder, Aran Banner, Skerry Champion, Ulster Chieftan, May Queen, etc.

Baked Potato Garnishing Ideas

Serve split baked Russets or Netted gems with their white flesh bursting through their skins. Arrange a plate of accompaniments, selecting from the following:

Dairy sour cream
dairy yogurt, plain
whipped butter
chopped scallions
chopped green onions or chives
minced parsley
caraway seeds
toasted sesame seeds
chopped dill
slivers of red onion

minced red and green peppers
sliced stuffed olives or ripe pitted
    black olives
crumbled fried bacon or salt pork
cracklings
grated Gruyère cheese
grated Parmesan cheese
crumbled blue cheese
chunks of Feta cheese
dabs of cream cheese

Baked Potato Toppings

Green Onion

1½ cups	plain yogurt	375 mL
2 tbsp.	chopped scallions	25 mL
1 tbsp.	tarragon vinegar	15 mL
1 tsp.	dry mustard	5 mL

Bacon Horseradish

½ cup	sour cream	125 mL
1 tsp.	grated horseradish	5 mL
6	slices cooked crumbled bacon	6

Blue Cheese

½ cup	sour cream	125 mL
½ cup	mayonnaise	125 mL
½ cup	crumbled blue cheese	125 mL
1 tbsp.	chopped parsley	15 mL

Cottage-Cheese-Stuffed Baked Potato

Overall timing: 1 hour   *Serves: 2*   *Calories: 160 per potato*

2	**small baking potatoes**	**2**
1	**small onion, chopped**	**1**
½ cup	**chicken stock**	**125 mL**
½ cup	**low-fat cottage cheese**	**125 mL**
1 tsp.	**chopped parsley**	**5 mL**
2 tbsp.	**grated Parmesan cheese**	**25 mL**
½ tsp.	**freshly ground pepper**	**2 mL**
2 tbsp.	**chopped chives**	**25 mL**

Bake potatoes. Slice potatoes off of tops and scoop out the centers. Simmer onion in chicken stock, then combine with potato pulp and other ingredients, except chives. Beat well. Fill potato shells, mound slightly and bake at 375°F (190°C) to heat. Microwave for 2 minutes on HIGH. Top with chives.

Swiss-Cheese-and-Ham-Stuffed Potato

Overall timing: 1 hour   *Serves: 4*   *Calories: 210 per potato*

4	**medium baking potatoes**	**4**
2 tbsp.	**sour cream**	**25 mL**
4 ozs.	**minced ham**	**115 g**
4 tbsp.	**grated Swiss cheese**	**60 ml**
1 tsp.	**salt**	**5 mL**
½ tsp.	**freshly ground pepper**	**2 mL**
	chopped chives	
	chopped parsley	
	fennel seeds	

Bake potatoes. Slice off tops of potatoes and scoop out the centers. Mix well with sour cream, ham, Swiss cheese, salt, and pepper. Sprinkle with chives, parsley, and fennel seeds. Bake at 375°F (190°C) until heated through, 8-10 minutes. Microwave on HIGH for 3-4 minutes.

Salmon Dill Potatoes

Overall timing: 1 hour   Serves: 4

4	baking potatoes, scrubbed	4
2 tbsp.	butter	25 mL
¼ cup	chicken broth	50 mL
1 cup	cooked flaked salmon	250 mL
2	large eggs, hard-boiled, chopped	2
⅓ cup	fresh dill or 1 tbsp. (15 mL) dried	75 mL
1 tsp.	onion flakes	5 mL

Bake potatoes, either in a microwave, for 15-18 minutes, or in a 425°F (220°C) oven for 45 minutes. Slice off tops, scoop out centers. Mix all ingredients together, do not beat. Mound filling in potato shells. Potatoes may be made ahead and refrigerated for up to 24 hours. Bake potatoes in a 400°F (200°C) oven for 15 minutes, 25 minutes if they are cold. Microwave should heat them in 5-8 minutes.

Yogurt-and-Cauliflower

Overall timing: 1 hour   Serves: 6

6	baking potatoes, scrubbed	6
2	medium onions, chopped	2
1½ cups	cauliflower florets, chopped	375 mL
2 tbsp.	butter	25 ml
1 tbsp.	curry powder	15 mL
cup	minced fresh parsley	125 mL
cup	plain yogurt	150 mL
tsp.	salt	2 mL
tsp.	pepper	1 mL

Bake potatoes, either in a microwave for 15-20 minutes, or in a 425°F (220°C) oven for 45 minutes. Slice off tops, and scoop out centers. While baking potatoes, lightly steam onions and cauliflower. Remove from heat and add all ingredients. Mix together well with potato pulp and mound in shells. Potatoes may be made ahead to this point and refrigerated for 24 hours. Bake potatoes in 400°F (200°C) oven for 15 minutes, 25 minutes if they are cold. Microwave should heat them in 10-12 minutes.

Shrimp or Crab Stuffing

Overall timing: 1 hour   *Serves: 6*

6	large baking potatoes	6
1 cup	cooked shrimp, or crab	250 g
¼ cup	chicken broth	50 mL
½ cup	onion, chopped	125 mL
1	clove garlic, crushed	1
1	egg	1
⅓ cup	chicken broth	75 mL
½ cup	scalded milk	125 mL
½ tsp.	salt	2 mL
¼ tsp.	freshly grated pepper	1 mL
½ cup	grated sharp Cheddar cheese	125 mL

Bake potatoes. Slice off tops of potatoes and scoop out the centers. Meanwhile, coarsely chop shrimp if they are large. In a skillet, heat the chicken broth. Sauté onion with garlic, shrimp or crab until onion is soft. Set aside. To potato pulp add egg, chicken broth, milk, salt, and pepper. Beat until smooth and fluffy. Stir in shrimp mixture and cheese. Fill each shell with potato mixture, mounding slightly. Bake in 400°F (200°C) oven for about 10 minutes, to heat through.

Stuffed Potatoes Chasseur

Overall timing: 1 hour   *Serves: 4*

4	baking potatoes, scrubbed	4
4-6	chicken livers, sliced	4-6
1 cup	fresh mushrooms, sliced	250 mL
2-3 tbsp.	butter	25-45 mL

Bake potatoes. Meanwhile, sauté chicken livers and mushrooms in butter until done, 5-8 minutes. Scoop pulp out of potatoes and mash. Mix half of potato with liver and mushroom mixtures. Refill shell, heat at 450°F (230°C) for 5 minutes. Serve with dabs of butter and chopped fresh parsley.

Curried-Egg-Stuffing

Overall timing: 1 hour   *Serves: 6*

6	medium baking potatoes	6
4	eggs, hard-boiled (keep 1 for garnish)	4
2 tbsp.	butter	25 mL
1	onion, minced	1
1	cooking apple, diced	1
2 tsp.	curry powder	10 mL
1 tsp.	salt	5 mL
½ tsp.	freshly ground pepper	2 mL
½ cup	milk	125 mL
	sprigs of parsley	

Bake potatoes. Finely chop 3 of the hard-boiled eggs. In butter sauté the egg, onion, apple, curry powder, salt, and pepper for 5 minutes. Scoop out the potato pulp and mix together with egg mixture and milk. Fill potato shells and reheat at 375°F (190°C) for 10 minutes or 2-3 minutes in the microwave. Garnish with egg slices and fresh parsley and serve immediately.

Bacon-and-Cheese-Stuffed Potatoes

Overall timing: 1 hour   *Serves: 6*   *Calories: 200 per potato*

6	medium baking potatoes	6
8	bacon rashers, chopped	8
½	onion, chopped	½
2 tsp.	marjoram	5 mL
2 tbsp.	sweet cream	25 mL
½ tsp.	salt	2 mL
¼ tsp.	white pepper	1 mL
¼ cup	grated sharp Cheddar cheese	50 mL

Bake potatoes. Meanwhile, cook bacon with onion, marjoram in a skillet. Scoop out potato pulp, mix with cream, salt, and pepper. Add bacon mixture, beat well. Refill potato shell, top with grated cheese. Broil for a few minutes to melt cheese; serve immediately.

Mexicali-Stuffed Potato

Overall timing: 1 hour   Serves: 6   Calories: 165 per potato

6	medium baking potatoes	6
1 cup	grated mozzarella cheese	250 mL
3	hot green chili peppers, chopped	3
½ cup	sour cream	125 mL
1 tsp.	salt	5 mL
½ tsp.	freshly ground pepper	2 mL
	sprigs of parsley	

Bake potatoes. Slice off tops and scoop out centers. Beat pulp together with ⅔ of the cheese. Add chili peppers, sour cream, salt, and pepper. Mound filling in shells. Sprinkle with remaining cheese. Bake at 350°F (180°C) for 15 minutes or microwave on HIGH for 5-7 minutes. Garnish with a sprig of parsley or more peppers. (These are quite HOT, cut back to 1 or 2 peppers if palate is cold!)

Yogurt-Vegetable-Stuffed Baked Potato

Overall timing: 1 hour   Serves: 2

2	medium baking potatoes	2
½ cup	chopped cooked spinach	125 mL
1	small carrot, finely chopped, cooked	1
1 tsp.	chives, chopped	5 mL
2 tbsp.	plain yogurt	25 mL
1 tsp.	vegetable flavoring (such as marmite)	5 mL
1 tbsp.	butter	15 mL

Bake potatoes. Slice off tops and scoop out centers. Mix all ingredients with potato pulp and stuff back into shell. Pop potato shells under hot grill for 3 minutes or microwave on HIGH for 1 minute. Serve hot with more chopped chives and another dab of yogurt.

Keep your vitamin C supply high — with potatoes.

Cheddar-Cheese-Stuffed Potato

Overall timing: *1 hour*   Serves: *2*   Calories: *217 per potato*

2	*medium baking potatoes*	*2*
¼ cup	*grated sharp Cheddar cheese*	*50 mL*
1 tbsp.	*plain yogurt*	*15 mL*
1	*small tomato, peeled and finely chopped*	*1*
1 tbsp.	*butter*	*15 mL*
½ tsp.	*salt*	*2 mL*
¼ tsp.	*white pepper*	*1 mL*
1 tsp.	*basil*	*5 mL*
	chopped chives or dill	

Bake potatoes. Slice off tops and scoop out pulp. Mix pulp with all ingredients except chives or dill, beat well. Refill potato shells and bake at 375°F (190°C) for 15 minutes. Microwave on HIGH for 3-5 minutes. Garnish with chives or dill.

Nutrition authorities say, reduce caloric intake but still include potatoes. Very few people can eat enough potatoes to make them fat!

Potatoes for the Barbecue

Overall timing: 35 minutes   *Serves: 6-8*

4	large baking potatoes	4
2	large onions	2
	butter	

Scrub potatoes, cut in half lengthwise. Cut a cross on cut portion, place a ¼" (1 cm) slice of onion on potato half and a dab of butter. Wrap in tin foil, place on grill on hot barbecue for 20-30 minutes, turning once.

Marinated Potatoes

Overall timing: Overnight, 30 minutes on barbecue   *Serves: 6-8*

| 4 | large baking potatoes | 4 |
| 1 cup | Italian salad dressing | 250 mL |

The night before, scrub and slice potatoes, cut into 1" (2.5 cm) lengthwise slices. Marinate in salad dressing overnight. Place on grill on hot barbecue, turn and brown on each side, until tender.
Delicious and different. No need to dress them up further.

SOUPS

This old-fashioned potato soup is one that I mastered at the age of 10. Saturday afternoons were spent "playing house" and cooking. Many a rainy afternoon I would cook this soup for my dear friend Linda, under Mother's supervision. The pot of soup was gingerly carried out to our playhouse, and there devoured with a great deal of ceremony and good manners.

Steaming, creamy, buttery soup.

German Butter Soup

Overall timing: 30 minutes   Serves: 4-6

1	bay leaf	1
8-10	black peppercorns	8-10
3	large potatoes, scrubbed, diced	3
1 tbsp.	chopped fresh parsley	15 mL
½ tsp.	salt	2 mL
¼ cup	macaroni	50 mL
1	onion, chopped	1
1 tbsp.	vinegar	15 mL
2 tbsp.	butter	25 mL
½ cup	cream	125 mL

Fill a 3-quart (3 L) saucepan with 4 cups (1 L) water. Place bay leaf and peppercorns in a spice basket, drop into water along with potatoes. Boil gently until potatoes are done. Add parsley, salt, macaroni, and onion, cook until macaroni is tender. Take off heat, add vinegar, butter, cream, and extra parsley. Remove spice basket.

NOTE: Add more butter to soup if you are not watching calories too closely.

The cooking technique of boiling was proven to be used as early as 5000 B.C., and was likely discovered by accident. (By dropping hot stones, from roaring fires, into potfuls of water. More hot stones were added to keep the water a suitable temperature — a prosaic occupation "sans doute".)

Aroostock County, Maine, U.S.A., for 30 years, until 1957, produced more potatoes than any other state. Farmers in those parts still claim they can feed a crew of 12 with 1 potato! They have a "Potato Blossom Festival", an annual event at which there are parades and festivities and a "Potato Queen" is chosen. Maine is presently seeking to revitalize its tired soil and improve potato varieties, while holding to traditional farming methods.

This potato soup, from Aroostock County, is also buttery and delicious.

Aroostock County Potato Soup

Overall timing: 1 hour   Serves: 4-6

7	small onions, thinly sliced	7
1 cup	thinly sliced celery	250 mL
6 tbsp.	butter	90 mL
4 cups	milk	1 L
2½ cups	diced boiling potatoes	625 mL
1½ tbsp.	white unbleached flour	22 mL
1 tsp.	salt	5 mL
½ tsp.	freshly ground pepper	2 mL
1 tbsp.	minced fresh parsley	15 mL

In top of double boiler over direct heat, sauté onion and celery in 4 tbsp. (60 mL) butter until golden. Add the milk and cook over boiling water for 45 minutes, stirring occasionally. Cook potato in boiling salted water for 10-15 minutes, drain. Heat remaining 2 tablespoons (25 mL) butter and blend in flour. Gradually stir in first mixture and potatoes. Cook until thickened. Add seasonings. Sprinkle with parsley before serving.

"You will need a queen-size pot to start this soup.

Potato and Sorrel Soup

Overall timing: 40 minutes   Serves: 6-8

6	large boiling potatoes	6
1 lb.	sorrel leaves (a BIG bunch)	500 g
1 tbsp.	butter	15 mL
1 cup	chopped onions	250 mL
6 cups	chicken broth	1.5 L
1 tbsp.	lemon juice	15 mL
1 tsp.	salt	5 mL
½ tsp.	freshly ground pepper	2 mL
1 cup	milk	250 mL

Chop the potatoes. Wash the sorrel leaves and remove heavy ribs running up the leaves. Slice leaves into very thin shreds. You should have 5-6 cups (1.25-1.56 L). Heat the butter and cook the onions until soft. Add the potatoes to the saucepan along with the broth and 3 cups (750 mL) of sorrel. Cook for 20 minutes or until the potatoes are soft, purée. Return to saucepan and reheat. Add lemon juice, salt, pepper, stir in remaining sorrel and cook until barely wilted. Add cream. Serve either very hot or chilled. Don't throw out the sorrel stems, tie them up and add them to the soup while it is cooking for added flavor. Remove before serving.

Genuine Goulash Soup

Overall timing: 40 minutes   Serves: 4-6

6	onions, sliced	6
3 tbsp.	bacon fat	45 mL
½ lb.	cubed boneless beef steak	250 g
2 tbsp.	ground paprika	25 mL
½ tsp.	pepper	2 mL
½ tsp.	marjoram leaves	2 mL
1 tsp.	salt	5 mL
3 cups	water	750 mL
5	tomatoes, skinned, chopped	5
2 cups	peeled, diced boiling potatoes	500 mL
1	green pepper, chopped	1
2	cloves of garlic, minced	2
½ cup	red wine	125 mL

Brown the onion slices in bacon fat. Add beef, spices, herbs, and salt. Stir, and continue to brown this mixture 10 minutes. As soon as enough meat juice has mixed with the fat in pan, pour on water, and let soup continue to cook over low heat. Add tomatoes, potatoes, green pepper, and cook gently for another 20 minutes. Add minced garlic and wine. Taste for seasoning, heat for 5 minutes and serve.

In prehistoric times it was woman's work to gather food such as edible greenstuffs, nuts, berries and edible roots. Protected from destruction by the soil, root vegetables must have always been important to early housewives. In Europe, turnips, carrots, and onions date back to prehistoric times. In the Americas it was the potato, along with a few other roots such as manioc, which survived the wars and rampages.

The infusion of a delectable tuber and a sweet root.

Potato and Carrot Soup Avec Créme

Overall timing: 30 minutes   Serves: 6

4	*large boiling potatoes, pared, diced*	*4*
4	*large carrots, peeled, sliced*	*4*
2	*small onions, chopped*	*2*
2 cups	*cream*	*500 mL*
1 tsp.	*salt*	*5 mL*
½ tsp.	*pepper, freshly ground*	*2 mL*
2 tbsp.	*chopped fresh parsley*	*25 ml*
	lemon juice	

Boil all vegetables in a small amount of water, until tender. Blend to purée. To purée add cream, salt, pepper. Reheat and spoon into bowls. Sprinkle with parsley to serve, and add a squeeze of lemon juice.

Navy Bean and Turkey Soup

Overall timing: 2 hours, 30 minutes   *Serves: 8-10*

1 cup	dry navy beans	250 mL
8 cups	water	2 L
2 tsp.	salt	10 mL
1	meaty turkey frame OR	1
1½ cups	chopped leftover turkey	375 mL
2	onions, chopped	2
2 tsp.	Worcestershire sauce	10 mL
½ tsp.	ground sage	2 mL
⅛ tsp.	pepper	0.5 mL
2 cups	chopped, cooked leftover potatoes	500 mL
1 cup	sliced celery	250 mL
1 cup	chopped turnip	250 mL

Rinse navy beans. In a 5-quart (5 L) Dutch oven, combine beans, water, and salt. Bring to a boil; reduce heat and simmer for 3 minutes. Remove from heat. Cover, let stand for 1 hour. DO NOT DRAIN. Break turkey frame to fit Dutch oven. Add to navy bean mixture. (If using chopped leftover turkey, add it when vegetables are cooked). Stir in onions, Worcestershire sauce, sage, and pepper. Cover and simmer 1 hour. Remove turkey frame; cool slightly. Cut meat off frame; chop meat. Slightly mash beans. Return meat to Dutch oven; add potatoes, celery, and turnip. Cover and simmer 20 minutes more. Serve with thick slices of French bread.

In 1795, American scientist, Benjamin Thompson decided upon a soup thickened with potatoes as a possible dish to feed the poor in Munich, "as well as possible", with "as little as possible". Potatoes were the main ingredient. It was some time before Mr. Thompson persuaded the poor of Munich to taste it but, shortly thereafter, people all over Germany favored potatoes, in soups at least.

A healthful soup filled with summer's bountiful garden fresh vegetables.

Mom's Potato Green Bean Soup

Overall timing: 40 minutes   *Serves: 6-8*

2 qts.	ham soup stock	2 L
2	onions, diced	2
2	large stalks celery diced	2
6 cups	fresh green beans, finely cut	2.5 L
2 cups	scrubbed, diced potatoes, preferably new potatoes	500 mL
3"x 2"	bundle fresh summer savory OR	(8 cm x 5 cm)
2 tsp.	dried summer savory	10 mL
½ tsp.	freshly ground pepper	2 mL
	sour cream — optional	

Add all vegetables to stock, simmer until vegetables are done, about ½ hour. 10 minutes before serving, add bundle of summer savory and pepper. Serve with a generous dollop of sour cream if you wish. (Don't forget to remove savory bundle.)

Potatoes are a good source of Vitamin K — which aids in the blood clotting process.

Did you know that in France there is an association of gourmets and chefs, who honor and promote the "pomme de terre", apple of the earth? It is called the "Academie Parmentier", named after the famous potato crusader, Auguste Parmentier.

A famous potato soup!

Hot Vichysoisse (or Cold)

Overall timing: 50 minutes   Serves: 6-8

4	*leeks*	4
4	*large boiling potatoes*	4
4	*chicken bouillon cubes*	4
1 tbsp.	*butter*	15 mL
1 cup	*cream*	250 mL
1 cup	*milk*	250 mL
½ cup	*potato leek liquid*	125 mL
¼ tsp.	*freshly ground pepper*	1 mL
1 tsp.	*salt*	5 mL
	chives	

Thoroughly wash leeks, chop into 1" (2.5 cm) pieces. Peel potatoes and chunk. Put in a saucepan, together with leeks, and cook with water until tender. Drain vegetables, reserve liquid. Pour into blender carafe and blend until puréed. You should have approximately ½ cup (125 mL) liquid left in pot. Pour into saucepan again and add ingredients, except chives, which you reserve to sprinkle on top of the soup. Heat and serve hot or very cold.

This soup is traditionally served cold but many palates prefer hot soup!

VARIATIONS:

Watercress Soup
— Omit leeks, replace with 2 cups (500 mL) chopped watercress, stir in another cup (250 mL) chopped watercress just before serving. Serve hot or very cold.

Jamaican Avocado
— Before serving, add ½ cup (125 ml) cooked peas, 1 avocado, sliced, and a dash of sherry peppers sauce, to the hot Vichysoisse.
— *You may purée the peas and avocado with other ingredients as you do for Vichysoisse.

A distinctive soup, with unusual "soup ingredients". A good time to use up lettuce when it is ready in the garden all at once.

Puréed Potato Yogurt Soup

Overall timing: 45 minutes   Serves: 6

3	medium boiling potatoes, peeled, cubed	3
1	cucumber, peeled, diced	1
5	green onions, including tops, sliced	5
3 cups	chopped lettuce	750 mL
½ tsp.	dill seed	2 mL
1	bay leaf	1
1 tbsp.	butter	15 mL
1 tsp.	salt	5 mL
¼ tsp.	pepper	1 mL
½ cup	plain yogurt	125 mL
1 cup	milk	250 mL
	Parmesan cheese	

Put all vegetables, dill seed and bay leaf in a large Dutch oven, cover with water and boil until potatoes are tender, about 25 minutes. Drain, remove bay leaf. In blender purée vegetables with butter, salt and pepper. Return to Dutch oven, add yogurt and milk. Heat but do not boil and serve, sprinkled with grated Parmesan cheese.

This is one of Mother's favorite recipes for borscht and it is truly a meal in a bowl. Other varieties are made with red beets instead of carrots and tomatoes. Another, variety the original Russian version, was comprised solely of vegetables, and loaded with butter and sour cream instead. You may wish to add more butter and sour cream to this recipe.

Russian Borscht with Meat

Overall timing: 3 hours, 30 minutes   Serves: 6-8

1	**small stewing chicken**	1
	OR	
1	**large meaty beef soup bone**	1
2 qts.	**water**	2 L
2	**large onions, chopped**	2
4	**boiling potatoes, pared, cubed**	4
4	**large carrots, sliced**	4
5 cups	**shredded cabbage**	1.25 L
2 tsp.	**salt**	10 mL
1 tsp.	**freshly ground pepper**	5 mL
½	**red chili pepper**	½
1	**1" x 6" (2.5 cm x 15 cm) bundle of fresh dill**	1
	OR	
2 tsp.	**dill seed**	10 mL
1 tbsp.	**chopped fresh parsley**	15 mL
2 cups	**chopped fresh tomatoes**	500 mL
1-2 tbsp.	**vinegar**	15-25 mL
2 tbsp.	**butter**	25 mL

Boil meat in a large Dutch oven for 2-3 hours. Remove bones and skim off fat. Add vegetables and spices, simmer until vegetables are done. Remove dill bundle and chili pepper. Before serving add vinegar, and butter. Serve with hot buttered white bread.

To vary, try adding chunks of smoked salmon in this soup in place of sausage.

Potato Sausage Soup

Overall timing: 40 minutes   Serves: 4

3	*large boiling potatoes, scrubbed, diced*	*3*
4 cups	*water*	*1 L*
½ lb.	*smoked sausage*	*250 g*
2	*large carrots*	*2*
2	*stalks celery*	*2*
1	*onion*	*1*
1 tsp.	*salt*	*5 mL*
½ tsp.	*pepper*	*2 mL*
1 tsp.	*thyme*	*5 mL*
1 cup	*milk*	*250 mL*

Prepare potatoes for boiling. Cut sausage into chunks and boil gently in water with potatoes, chopped vegetables, and seasonings. Cook until vegetables are done. Add milk to serve.

Clam Chowder

Overall timing: 1 hour   Serves: 4-6

4	*strips bacon*	*4*
1 tsp.	*thyme*	*5 mL*
2	*onions, chopped*	*2*
48 oz.	*Clamato juice*	*1.36 L*
2 cups	*cooked clams*	*500 mL*
4	*boiling potatoes, pared, diced*	*4*
4	*stalks celery, sliced*	*4*
4	*carrots, peeled, sliced*	*4*
1 tsp.	*salt*	*5 mL*
½ tsp.	*freshly ground pepper*	*2 mL*
1-2 tbsp.	*chopped fresh parsley*	*15-25 mL*
⅛ tsp.	*sherry pepper sauce*	*0.5 mL*
	cornstarch for thickening	

Chop bacon and brown in a large Dutch oven. Add ½ tsp. (2 mL) thyme to onions and sauté until soft. Add clamato juice, clams, other vegetables and spices. Simmer until vegetables are done. Thicken with a little cornstarch mixed with water. Add more parsley to serve. Fresh clams from lake or sea are the ultimate in this soup, of course.

New England Fish Chowder

Overall timing: 50 minutes   Serves: 4-6

6 oz.	salt pork	170 g
6	boiling potatoes, pared	6
4 tbsp.	butter	60 mL
2 cups	chopped onions	500 mL
2 cups	chopped celery	500 mL
6 cups	water	1.5 L
1 tsp.	salt	5 mL
½ tsp.	freshly ground pepper	2 mL
2 lb.	whitefish such as cod, bass, haddock, boned	1 kg
2 cups	light cream	500 mL
3 tbsp.	chopped fresh parsley	45 mL

Cut salt pork into ¼" pieces and blanch for 5 minutes in boiling water. Drain and pat dry. Dice potatoes and place in cold water until ready to use. In saucepan, sauté salt pork until it is lightly browned and the fat is rendered. Discard fat, add butter, onions, celery, and sauté 8-10 minutes. Add potatoes and water, bring to a boil and simmer about 15 minutes. Season.

Cut fish into chunks and add to pan. The fish will be cooked in a few minutes. Then add cream, heat and taste for seasoning and sprinkle with parsley to serve.

*Sprinkle shrimp on top of soup for added color and flavor.

Nutritionists say that potatoes are predominantly an alkaline food.

A potato hint:
Save your oversalted soup or stew. A raw potato dropped into an oversalted soup or stew will absorb much of the salt taste. Cook for about ½ an hour then discard the potato.

A hearty meal.

Potato Soup with Poached Eggs

Overall timing: 1 hour   Serves: 6

2	onions, chopped	2
1	leek, chopped	1
1 tbsp.	olive oil	15 mL
4	large boiling potatoes, pared, sliced	4
2	cloves garlic, crushed	2
6 cups	beef stock	1.5 L
1	bay leaf	1
1 tsp.	thyme	5 mL
½ tsp.	fennel	2 mL
⅛ tsp.	saffron	0.5 mL
2 tbsp.	dried orange peel	25 mL
1 tsp.	salt	5 mL
½ tsp.	freshly ground pepper	2 mL
1 tbsp.	chopped fresh parsley	15 mL
6	large eggs	6
6	chunky slices of toast	6

Brown onions and leeks in olive oil. Add potatoes, garlic, and the next 8 ingredients. Boil together gently, uncovered, about 20 minutes. Take out potatoes and keep hot. Lower flame and poach eggs in soup broth for 3 minutes. Drain eggs and place on a platter. Make toast and place on individual serving dishes. Pour soup broth over toast. Place potatoes and poached eggs on top and sprinkle with parsley. Serve immediately.

BREADS AND YEAST ROLLS

In a town on the island of P.E.I., a tiny farming community called O'Leary, people get ready for a "Potato Blossom Festival" the end of July. The festival is scheduled so that it coincides with the week that potato fields will be in bloom. O'Leary and neighbouring areas have good reason to celebrate — they grow world-renowned, first-class potatoes! Potatoes and fish have long been a staple here.

Bannock made with mashed potatoes is one bread that goes well with seafood.

Potato Bannock

Overall timing: 30 minutes   *Makes: 12-16*

2½ cups	unbleached white flour	625 mL
2 tbsp.	baking powder	25 mL
1 tbsp.	sugar	15 mL
1 tsp.	salt	5 mL
⅓ cup	butter	75 mL
1 cup	milk	250 mL
1 cup	cold mashed potatoes (may be leftovers)	250 mL
1 tbsp.	milk	15 mL

In a large bowl, combine flour, baking powder, sugar, and salt. Cut in butter until mixture resembles coarse crumbs. With a fork, stir in 1 cup (250 mL) milk and potatoes. Transfer to lightly floured surface and knead gently, 3 or 4 times, working in a little extra flour if dough is too sticky.

Place dough on an ungreased cookie sheet and pat with hands to form a large oval, about 1" (2.5 cm) thick. Brush with milk and bake at 450°F (230°C) until golden, about 15 minutes. Slice and serve with butter. Nice with soup, chowder, or stew.

VARIATION:
— Add 1 tbsp. (15 mL) chopped fresh dill.
— Add 1 cup (250 mL) chopped alfalfa sprouts, reducing milk about a ¼ cup (50 mL).

Experiment with your favorite recipes, by adding a small amount of mashed potato, ½ to 1 cup (125 mL-250 mL) to begin. Adding mashed potatoes adds nutrients, a soft texture, and helps to retain moisture in your baked goods.

This bread is high in vitamins, protein, and fibre.

Country Style Potato Rye Bread

Overall timing: 3 hours   Makes 4 loaves

4 cups	potato water	1 L
3 tsp.	brown sugar	15 mL
2 tbsp.	active dry yeast	25 mL
1 cup	mashed potatoes (may be leftovers)	250 mL
5 cups	unbleached white flour	1.25 L
2 tsp.	salt	10 mL
3 cups	rye flour	750 mL
1½ cups	bran	375 mL
½ cup	wheat germ	125 mL
½ cup	soy flour	125 mL
¼ cup	soft butter	50 mL

To 4 cups (1 L) of lukewarm potato water, add and dissolve sugar. Sprinkle on yeast, do not stir. When yeast puffs up and softens about 10 minutes, stir well and beat in mashed potatoes, 5 cups (1.25 L) white flour, salt. Set bowl in warm water and cover. Let rise about 25 minutes, then work in rye flour, bran, wheat germ, soy flour, also adding butter. Knead about 15 minutes or until smooth. Let rise until double in bulk, setting bowl in warm place, covered. Shape into 4 loaves, let rise ½ hour or so in greased pans. Does not have to be double in size. Bake in a preheated oven at 400°F (200°C) for 45-50 minutes. Turn out of pan to cool.

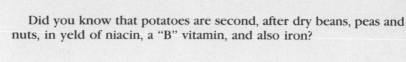

Did you know that potatoes are second, after dry beans, peas and nuts, in yeld of niacin, a "B" vitamin, and also iron?

White Potato Bread

Overall timing: 3 hours   Makes: 3 loaves

2	*medium boiling potatoes, pared*	*2*
½ cup	*potato water*	*125 mL*
2 tbsp.	*sugar (divided)*	*25 mL*
2 tbsp.	*active dry yeast*	*25 mL*
4 tbsp.	*butter*	*60 mL*
1½ cups	*warm cream*	*375 mL*
1 tbsp.	*salt*	*15 mL*
6-7½ cups	*white unbleached flour*	*1.5 L*

Dice potatoes. Cook in 2 cups (500 mL) water until soft. Drain potatoes, reserving liquid. If necessary, add hot tap water to potato liquid to make ½ cup (125 mL). Stir 1 tbsp. (15 mL) sugar into potato water and cool to lukewarm. Then sprinkle in yeast. Let stand for 10 minutes. Mash potatoes with a mixer in a large bowl and add butter, cream, salt and remaining sugar. Mix until butter is melted. Add yeast mixture and 4 cups (1 L) flour. Stir until well blended. Stir in additional flour to make a stiff dough, about 2 more cups (500 mL). Turn out on a lightly floured surface, kneading in more flour as necessary. Knead until smooth and elastic, about 10 minutes. Place dough in a bowl greased with butter. Cover and let rise until double in volume, about 1 hour. Punch dough down, turn out on to lightly floured surface, knead in another ½-1 cup (125 mL-250 mL) flour. Divide and shape into loaves. Cover and let rise until doubled in size, about 1 hour. Sprinkle loaves with flour or seeds. Bake at 400°F (200°C) for 45 minutes or until golden brown.

Makes a nice chewy bread, delicious toasted!

I shy away from foods which carry additives, doing so should promote better health across our nation in the future. I use unbleached flour whenever possible because less nutrients have been artifically removed.

In breads and yeast doughs, always try to use leftover potato water, it contains vitamins and minerals and is another way to "add" to a healthy bread.

Did you know that potatoes produce a higher yield per acre of land, at less cost, than grain, and need no processing after harvesting, which makes them an economical buy?

When you are in the mood for fussing, "chewy" and delicious with cream cheese.

Water Potato Bagels

Overall timing: 3 hours   Makes: 1 dozen

½ cup	warm potato water	125 mL
1 tsp.	white sugar	5 mL
1 tbsp.	active dry yeast	15 mL
1½ cups	warm potato water	375 mL
4 tbsp.	white sugar	60 mL
2 tsp.	salt	10 mL
5-6 cups	unbleached white flour	1.25-1.5 L
1 cup	cold mashed potatoes (may be leftovers)	250 mL
1	egg white, beaten	1
1 tbsp.	cold water	15 mL

Measure ½ cup (125 mL) warm potato water into a large bowl. Stir in 1 tsp. (5 mL) sugar and dry yeast. Let stand 10 minutes, then stir well. Meantime combine 1½ cups (375 mL) warm potato water, 4 tbsp. (60 mL) sugar, salt. Add to dissolved yeast. Add 1½ cups (375 mL) flour, mashed potatoes and beat until smooth. Stir in an additional 4 cups (1 L) flour or so to make a soft dough. Turn out onto lightly floured board and knead until smooth and elastic, about 10 minutes. Place in an ungreased bowl, cover and let rise in a warm place for ½-¾ of an hour. Dough will not be doubled in bulk. Punch dough down. Turn onto lightly floured board, roll dough into 12" x 10" (30 cm x 25 cm) rectangle. Cut dough into 12 equal strips. 1" x 10" (2.5 cm x 25 cm) each. Pinch ends of strip together to form a circle. Place on ungreased baking sheets. Cover and let rise in a warm place for ½ hour. Dough will not double in bulk.

Boil a 2" (5 cm) depth of water in 2 large shallow pans. Lower heat and add bagels, a few at a time. Simmer gently for 8 minutes. Remove from water and place on a towel to cool. Cool 5 minutes. Place on ungreased baking sheets. Bake at 350°F (180°C) for 10-12 minutes. Remove from oven, brush with combined egg white and water. Return to oven, bake for another 15 minutes or until golden brown. Cool on wire racks. To serve, split and fill with cream cheese and/or with smoked lox or butter.

Rich in spices and dried fruits this is a Hot Cross loaf with a difference.

Hot Cross Loaf

Overall timing: 3 hours, 30 minutes   *Makes: 3 loaves*

⅔ cup	milk	150 mL
1 cup	sugar	250 mL
1 tsp.	salt	5 mL
⅔ cup	soft butter	150 mL
1 cup	mashed potatoes (may be leftovers)	250 mL
⅔ cup	lukewarm potato water	150 mL
2 tsp.	sugar	10 mL
2 tbsp.	active dry yeast	25 mL
3	eggs, well beaten	3
2 tsp.	cinnamon	10 mL
1 tsp.	nutmeg	5 mL
½ tsp.	mace	2 mL
6 cups	sifted unbleached white flour (approx.)	1.5 L
1 cup	raisins	250 mL
1 cup	currants	250 mL
½ cup	mixed peel	125 mL
1 cup	chopped dried apricots	250 mL
1	slightly beaten egg yolk	1
2 tbsp.	water	25 mL

Icing:

⅔ cup	icing sugar	150 mL
½ tsp.	vanilla	2 mL
1	egg white	1

Grease 3 medium loaf pans. Scald milk and stir in white sugar, salt, butter, and mashed potaotes. Cool to lukewarm. Meantime, measure water in a lukewarm 4-quart (1 L) bowl, stir in 2 tsp. (10 mL) sugar, and sprinkle with yeast. Let stand 10 minutes, then stir well. Add potato mixture and well-beaten eggs. Mix spices into 3 cups (750 mL) of the flour and stir into yeast mixture, beat until smooth. Stir in raisins, currants, peel, chopped apricots. Stir in additional flour, about 4 cups (1 L) to make a stiff dough. Turn out on a floured board and knead until smooth and elastic.

Hot Cross Loaf (cont'd)

Place in a greased bowl, grease top, and cover. Let rise in a warm place until double in bulk, about 1¼ hours. Punch dough down and turn on lightly floured board. Divide dough into 3 equal parts or portions, cover with a tea towel, and let rest 10 minutes. Shape each portion of dough into a loaf and place in a prepared pan. Brush tops with a mixture of lightly beaten egg yolk and water. Cover and let rise in a warm place, until double in bulk, about 50 minutes.

Bake at 350°F (180°C) for 35-40 minutes. Turn out of pan and cool before icing. Measure icing sugar into a bowl, blend in vanilla and sufficient egg white to moisten. Drop icing from the tip of a spoon to make crosses on top of loaf, sprinkle with colored sugar.

Potato Refrigerator Rolls

Overall timing: 3 hours, 30 minutes   *Makes: 3-4 dozen*

2 tsp.	yeast	25 mL
2½ cups	lukewarm potato water	625 mL
⅔ cup	shortening (part butter for flavor)	150 mL
½ cup	honey	125 mL
1½ tsp.	salt	7 mL
1 cup	lukewarm mashed potatoes	250 mL
2	eggs, well beaten	2
7-8 cups	unbleached white flour	1.75-2 L
	melted butter	
	poppy seeds or sesame seeds (optional)	

Sprinkle yeast into 1½ cups (375 mL) of the potato water. In a mixing bowl, cream fats, and honey, salt, mashed potatoes. Blend eggs into yeast mixture. Blend egg-yeast mixture into creamed mix. Add remaining 1 cup (250 mL) water. Add flour gradually, mixing it thoroughly. With hands work in more flour until the dough is no longer sticky and is possible to handle. Knead 10 minutes. Set to rise in a greased bowl. When doubled in bulk, about 2 hours, take out amount needed for baking, punch down the remainder, cover with foil and refrigerate. Can be stored for 3 weeks, in refrigerator.

Shape rolls and brush with melted butter, or dip into poppy seeds or sesame seeds. Let rolls rise in a warm place, covered, until double in size. Bake at 425°F (220°C) 15-18 minutes.

Potato Croissants

Overall timing: 4 hours   Makes: 24 rolls

¾ cup	softened butter	175 mL
¼ cup	unsifted unbleached white flour	50 mL
½ cup	warm potato water	125 mL
1 tsp.	white sugar	5 mL
1 tbsp.	active dry yeast	15 mL
¾ cup	milk	175 mL
3 tbsp.	white sugar	45 mL
1 tsp.	salt	5 mL
1	egg, beaten	1
½ cup	warm mashed potatoes	125 mL
2½-2¾ cups	unbleached white flour	625-650 mL
1	egg	1
1 tbsp.	milk	15 mL
	sugar	

Cut butter into a ¼ cup (50 mL) flour until smooth and pasty. Place between waxed paper and roll into a 10" x 4" (25 cm x 10 cm) rectangle. Chill 1 hour. Meanwhile prepare dough. Measure ½ cup (125 mL) warm potato water into a large bowl. Stir in 1 tsp. (5 mL) sugar and yeast. Let stand 10 minutes, stir well. Heat milk over low until warm, stir in 3 tbsp. (45 mL) sugar and the salt. Add liquid to dissolved yeast, add beaten egg, ½ cup (125 mL) mashed potatoes. Put mixture through sieve if it is lumpy. Add ¾ cup (175 mL) flour. Beat until smooth. Stir in additional flour to make a soft dough. Turn onto a heavily floured board. Roll out to a 12" (30 cm) square. Carefully peel paper away from chilled butter mixture, place over center ⅓ of dough. Fold an outside ⅓ of dough over butter slab, then cover with remaining ⅓ of dough. Give dough a quarter turn. Roll out to 12" (30 cm) square. Fold again as above. Turn dough, roll and fold as above 3 more times. Wrap in waxed paper, chill for 2 hours.

Divide dough into 3 pieces, shape 1 piece at a time, refrigerate the remainder. Roll dough on floured board into a 12" (30 cm) circle. Cut into 8 pie-shaped pieces. Beat 1 egg, milk, and brush points with mixture. Roll up tightly, beginning at wide end. Seal points. Place on greased baking sheet with points underneath. Curve to form croissants. Brush with egg mixture, sprinkle with sugar, let rise uncovered in a warm place, free from draft, until high and light. Bake at 375°F (190°C) about 12 minutes, until golden brown.

Nice served hot. They freeze well too!

Serve with gourmet coffee and your favorite preserves. Close your eyes, pretend you're having breakfast at Maxims, 3 Rue Royale, Paris.

Potatoes supply us with amino acids, important growth nutrients for children! A recent poll indicated that potatoes were equally as well liked by children as was pizza.

Potato "Refrigerator Roll" Pizza

Overall timing: 1 hour, 30 minutes   Serves: 4

⅓	**recipe of Potato Refrigerator Roll dough, page 141.**	*⅓*
1½ cups	**seasoned tomato sauce**	*375 mL*
½ cup	**grated Parmesan cheese**	*125 mL*
1 lb.	**browned ground beef, or**	*500 g*
10	**pieces sliced ham, or**	*10*
1 cup	**cooked shrimp, or,**	*250 mL*
½ lb.	**pepperoni slices**	*250 g*
1	**green onion, chopped**	*1*
½	**green pepper, thinly sliced**	*½*
½ cup	**pineapple chunks**	*125 mL*
1 cup	**grated melting cheese, (mozzarella)**	*250 mL*

Take ⅓ of potato dough recipe out of refrigerator, let sit in a warm place for 1 hour, covered. Grease a pizza pan, then spread dough to fit. Preheat oven to 450°F (230°C). No need to let dough rise. Pour ½ of the sauce on dough, sprinkle with Parmesan cheese. Top with meat, rest of sauce, then add onions, peppers, pineapple or other toppings. Top with more Parmesan cheese. Bake for 10-12 minutes, then top with a good melting cheese. Pop back into oven to melt cheese. Cut into wedges to serve.

Other Pizza Toppings:
— chopped cooked artichokes
— black or green olives
— sliced tomatoes
— sliced mushrooms
— anchovy fillets
— sliced salami
— grated raw carrots
— chopped roasted chestnuts
— steamed cold spinach

Cinnamon Raisin Rolls

Overall timing: 2 hours, 30 minutes   *Makes: 12 rolls*

⅓	recipe of Potato Refrigerator Roll dough, page 141.	⅓
¼ cup	melted butter	50 mL
½ cup	brown sugar	125 mL
¼ cup	raisins	50 mL
2 tsp.	cinnamon	10 mL

Take out amount of dough needed for rolls. Let sit in a warm place, covered, for 1 hour. Then proceed with recipe.

Roll dough out to a 12" x 8" (30 cm x 20 cm) rectangle, ½" (1.3 cm) thick. Spread with melted butter, brown sugar, raisins, cinnamon. Roll up lengthwise, make 12, 1" (2.5 cm) slices. Place slices on a greased cookie sheet or in a muffin tin. Let rise in a warm place, covered, until double in bulk. Bake for 15-20 minutes at 375°F (190°C).

Walnut Danish

Overall timing: 2 hours, 30 minutes   *Makes: 24*

⅓	recipe of Potato Refrigerator Roll dough, page 141.	⅓

Maple Icing:

½ cup	butter	125 mL
1 cup	brown sugar	250 mL
¼ cup	milk	50 mL
2 cups	icing sugar	500 mL
1 cup	finely crushed walnuts	250 mL

Take out ⅓ of potato refrigerator roll dough. Let sit in a warm place, covered, for 1 hour. Roll out a piece about 12" x 12" (30 cm x 30 cm) and cut into ½" (1.3 cm) strips. Twist strips, make a circle with strip, pinch end of dough to side and place on a cookie sheet to rise. Let rise until double in bulk, bake at 375°F (190°C) for 15 minutes. Cool, in meantime make icing.

To make Maple Icing, melt butter in a saucepan, add brown sugar and milk. Boil over low heat 2 minutes stirring constantly. Cool to lukewarm. Gradually add 1¾ to 2 cups (425-500 mL) icing sugar. Beat until thick enough to spread. If icing becomes too stiff, add a little hot water. Ice immediately, dip into crushed walnuts.

DESSERTS AND SWEETS

This recipe for a cake has to be the ultimate in a chocolate torte. The mashed potatoes make it moist and the addition of spices creates a rare refinement. It won first prize in an "Alaskan cake contest" and rates first class everywhere it goes.

Potato Torte

Overall timing: 1 hour, 15 minutes   *Serves: 8-10*

1 cup	butter	250 mL
1½ cups	brown sugar	375 mL
4	eggs, beaten	4
½ cup	cold mashed potatoes (not leftovers)	125 mL
1 cup	milk	250 mL
2½ cups	unbleached white flour	625 mL
2 tsp.	baking powder	10 mL
½ tsp.	salt	2 mL
2 tsp.	cinnamon	10 mL
1 tsp.	allspice	5 mL
½ cup	melted chocolate, 4 oz. (115 g) unsweetened chocolate (do not use cocoa)	125 mL
½ cup	finely chopped walnuts	125 mL
1 tsp.	vanilla	5 mL
¼-½ cup	flaked almonds for decoration	50-125 mL

Butter 2, 9" (23 cm) or 10" (25 cm) round baking tins. Begin by creaming butter, then add sugar and eggs, beating well after each addition. Add mashed potatoes and milk, then stir this mixture into creamed butter/mixture. Sift flour with baking powder, salt, and spices. Add to butter mixture. Melt chocolate in a double boiler, then stir it into butter mixture. Add walnuts and vanilla, beat well. Pour batter into 2 prepared pans, and bake at 350°F (180°C) for 45-50 minutes. You may test for doneness with a toothpick, when the toothpick comes out clean, the cake is done. Cool 10 minutes, then tip cakes out of pan and continue cooling on a wire rack. Ice when completely cooled.

Orange Icing:

3 tbsp.	melted butter	45 mL
3 tbsp.	thawed frozen orange juice concentrate	45 mL
2 cups	icing sugar	500 mL

Beat ingredients for 2 minutes with a mixer, then ice cake. You may use icing between layers or fill with strawberry or raspberry jam. Surround the top with almonds.

146

"Seedy Cakes" originated in England. A taste treat to be sure!

Potato Seedy Cake

Overall timing: 50 minutes   *Serves: 8-10*

1½ cups	sifted unbleached white flour	375 mL
¾ cup	white sugar	175 mL
2 tsp.	baking powder	10 mL
½ tsp.	salt	2 mL
½ tsp.	ground allspice	2 mL
1 tsp.	caraway seeds	5 mL
¼ cup	butter	50 mL
1 cup	dried currants	250 mL
1 cup	cold mashed potatoes (may be leftovers)	250 mL
2	eggs, well beaten	2
¼-½ cup	milk, if too thick	50-125 mL

Sift dry ingredients, stir in caraway seeds. Rub in butter, mix well. Add remaining ingredients, beat well. If very stiff, add milk. Bake in a greased 8" x 8" (20 cm x 20 cm) pan, in 425°F (220°C) oven for 30 minutes.

Fen Country Gold Cake

Overall timing: 1 hour   *Serves: 6*

4	large boiling potatoes, pared, cooked	4
⅔ cup	sugar	150 mL
½ cup	finely chopped candied peel	125 mL
⅓ cup	melted butter	75 mL
1 tsp.	vanilla	5 ml
2	eggs	2
½ cup	rich cream	125 mL
½ cup	white sugar (for top)	125 mL

Grease a 10" (25 cm) glass pie plate. Rice or sieve hot cooked potatoes into a bowl. Stir in sugar, peel, butter, and vanilla. Separate eggs and add beaten egg yolks to mixture. Gently fold stiffly beaten egg whites and cream into mixture. Turn batter into the prepared pie plate, smooth top and bake at 350°F (180°C) for 40-50 minutes. Baking time depends on wetness of potatoes used. Cake should be nicely browned and tester should come out clean. Turn out carefully onto a serving dish. The cake is soft and fragile. Sprinkle with another ½ cup (125 mL) sugar, serve hot.

Bay Potato Bars

Overall timing: 1 hour   Makes: 36 squares

½ cup	soft butter	125 mL
⅛ cup	white sugar	25 mL
4 tbsp.	cocoa	60 mL
1	egg	1
1½ cups	crushed All-Bran cereal	375 mL
1½ cups	fine unsweetened coconut	375 mL
½ cup	chopped walnuts	125 mL
6 tbsp.	hot mashed potatoes	90 mL
3 cups	icing sugar	750 mL
½ tsp.	bitter almond flavoring or vanilla	2 mL
1-2 tsp.	milk, if too thick	5-10 mL
1 cup	semisweet chocolate chips	250 mL
1 tsp.	butter	5 mL

Mix first 4 ingredients. Cook over boiling water, until thickened. Do not overcook or it will separate. Take off heat, add cereal, coconut, nuts. Blend, press into an 8" (20 cm) square pan.

Prepare mashed potatoes and mix well with icing sugar, flavoring, and a little milk, if needed. Spread filling over crust. Chill 5 minutes.

Melt chocolate over hot water, add butter, blend. Spread chocolate over filling immediately. Work quickly as chocolate hardens quickly. Mark into squares before chocolate hardens, to prevent cracks when cutting. Refrigerate until ready to use. Keeps well.

Potato Bars

Overall timing: 45 minutes   Makes: 1½ dozen squares

½ cup	packed, riced, boiled potato, cooled	125 mL
2 cups	icing sugar, (more or less needed)	500 mL
1 cup	coarsely chopped hazelnuts	250 mL
½ tsp.	salt	2 mL
7 oz.	pkg. unsweetened shredded coconut	200 g
1 tsp.	vanilla	5 mL
1 tsp.	butter	5 mL
8 oz.	dark semisweet chocolate	250 g

In a bowl combine all but chocolate. Press into 8" x 8" (20 cm x 20 cm) pan. Melt chocolate over double boiler, spread over potato mixture, sprinkle with a few chopped hazelnuts, chill. Cut candy bars into squares. Keeps, individually wrapped and chilled, 1 week.

Glazed Potato Doughnuts

Overall timing: 3-4 hours   *Makes: 6-7 dozen*

2 tsp.	white sugar	10 mL
1 cup	potato water, lukewarm	250 mL
2 tbsp.	yeast	25 mL
5	eggs	5
1 cup	sugar	250 mL
4 cups	cream	1 L
1 cup	soft butter	250 mL
1½ tsp.	salt	7 mL
2 cups	cold mashed potatoes (may be leftovers)	500 mL
16-20 cups	unbleached white flour	4-5 L

Dissolve sugar in lukewarm water, sprinkle yeast over. Meanwhile, beat eggs until fluffy, gradually beating in sugar. Scald cream, remove from heat, stir in soft butter, salt, mashed potatoes. Then stir yeast mixture and add to potato mixture. Stir in 16 cups (4 L) of flour, to make a soft dough, adding more if needed.

Knead dough until elastic, 15 minutes. Cover and let rise 1½ hours in a warm place (oven, with the light on.) Punch dough down, then let rise again for ½-¾ hour. Divide dough into 4 pieces, roll out a piece at a time to ½" (1.3 cm) thickness. Cut out doughnuts. Place on cookie sheet, cover and let rise again until double in size.

Deep-fry in 350°F (180°C) fat, turning as soon as they rise, (prevents cracking) until golden on both sides. Glaze, (see recipe below).

Glaze

1 cup	icing sugar	250 mL
2 tsp.	vanilla or	10 mL
2 tbsp.	orange, or pineapple juice, or water	30 mL

Absolutely scrumpdillicious, these potato doughnuts will surely become stand-ard fare at your home as they are at mine! Remember to keep the dough light, try to use as little flour as possible when rolling, and flip them over as soon as they rise. Good luck.

Cake Potato Doughnuts

Overall timing: 1 hour, 30 minutes   *Makes: 3 dozen*

2 cups	warm mashed potatoes (may be leftovers)	500 mL
3 tbsp.	cooking oil	45 mL
3	large eggs	3
1 cup	sweet milk	250 mL
5 cups	cake and pastry flour	1.25 L
1½ cups	sugar	375 mL
5 tsp.	baking powder	25 mL
1 tsp.	salt (reduce if you've used leftover potatoes)	5 mL
1 tsp.	nutmeg	5 mL

Prepare mashed potatoes and cool to lukewarm. Beat well, potatoes, oil, eggs, milk. Sift dry ingredients and mix lightly with first mixture. Make a soft dough. It may still be somewhat sticky inside when rolled. On a floured board, roll dough to ½" (1.3 cm) thickness. With a well-floured doughnut cutter, cut out doughnuts. Heat oil to 375°F (190°C) in a deep-fryer, oil depth should be at least 3" (7 cm). Drop doughnuts into hot fat carefully, so as not to splash! As soon as doughnuts rise in fat, turn over, then turn over again when second side is golden. Drain on paper towels or brown paper, sprinkle with sugar and/or cinnamon, or ice when doughnuts are cool. Dip in coconut, chocolate sprinkles, or chopped nuts, as you wish.

Potatoes contain iron, nearly 100% available for the body's diges-tion — an important factor for women to remember.

In 1980, as many as 5 billion pounds of French Fries were con-sumed by Americans.

150

Potato Tea Biscuits

Overall timing: 35 minutes   Serves: 4

1 cup	riced boiling potatoes	250 mL
1½ cups	unbleached white flour	375 mL
4 tsp.	baking powder	20 mL
½ tsp.	salt	2 mL
4 tbsp.	butter	60 mL
½ cup	milk (more or less, to make a soft dough)	125 mL

Pare and cut into quarters, 2-3 small boiling potatoes. Cook in a small amount of water until soft. Meanwhile, sift flour with baking powder and salt. Cut in butter and mix until crumbly. Drain and rice potatoes. Cool. Lightly mix cooled rice potato with flour mixture. Add cold milk.

Turn out on a floured board. Lightly roll or pat out and cut out in rectangles or rounds. Bake on a greased pan in 450°F (230°C) oven for 15-20 minutes. Serve hot!

Spiced Potato Muffins

Overall timing: 40 minutes   Makes: 1 dozen

1½ cups	sifted whole-wheat flour	375 mL
3 tsp.	baking powder	15 mL
2 tsp.	baking soda	10 mL
½ tsp.	salt	2 mL
¼ tsp.	each nutmeg, ginger, mace	1 mL
¾ cup	brown sugar	175 mL
1	large egg	1
½ cup	buttermilk or sour milk	125 mL
⅓ cup	vegetable oil	75 mL
½ tsp.	vanilla	2 mL
1½ cups	finely grated potato	375 mL
¼ cup	currants	50 mL
½ cup	raisins	125 mL
½ cup	chopped nuts	125 mL

Measure and sift together dry ingredients. Beat together egg, milk, oil, vanilla, potato. Stir currants, raisins, nuts into dry ingredients. Add wet ingredients and mix lightly with a fork. Batter will be dry. Fill muffin tin cups ¾ full. Bake at 400°F (200°C) for 17-20 minutes.

Try mashed potatoes in cookies!
In Dardilly, France, the headmaster of a cooking school requires his students to prepare 60 potato dishes before graduation.

For these potato pecan cookies, you may have to grind or pulverize stars of star aniseed and the blender works well for this.

Potato Pecan Cookies

Overall timing: 1 hour   Makes: 3 dozen

½ cup	softened butter	125 mL
¾ cup	brown sugar	175 mL
1	large egg	1
1 tsp.	vanilla	5 mL
¼ cup	ground pecans	50 mL
¾ cup	hot mashed potatoes	175 mL
1¼ cups	unbleached white flour	300 mL
½ tsp.	ground star aniseed	2 mL
½ tsp.	soda	2 mL
¼ tsp.	salt	1 mL
	whole pecans	

Cream butter, adding sugar a little at a time. Add egg, beat well. Add vanilla, ground pecans, hot mashed potato and beat well. Sift together flour and spices and add to butter mixture. Roll into 1" (2.5 cm) balls. Roll in white sugar if you wish. Place on cookie sheet, place ¼ or ½ of a pecan in the center and press down lightly. Bake at 350°F (180°C) for 10-12 minutes or until lightly browned. Cool on rack and store in a cool cupboard or refrigerator.

Apricot-Potato Dessert Dumplings

Overall timing: 1 hour   Serves: 8-10

4	*large boiling potatoes, boiled in skins*	4
5 tbsp.	*unbleached white flour*	75 mL
4	*egg yolks*	4
3 tbsp.	*melted butter*	45 mL
½ tsp.	*salt*	2 mL
25	*apricots, pitted*	25
25	*sugar cubes, doused in brandy*	25
2 tbsp.	*butter*	25 mL
1-2 tbsp.	*icing sugar*	15-25 mL
½ cup	*bread crumb, toasted in butter*	125 mL

Mash the peeled, boiled potatoes with a potato masher or run through the ricer. The purée should be dry and free of lumps. Mix with the flour, egg yolks, melted butter, salt. Knead these ingredients into a smooth dough, fashion it into a thick cord and slice this into thick slices. Remove the pits from the apricots and replace them with lumps of sugar moistened with brandy. Wrap the dough slices around the apricots, enclosing them completely. Cook the dumplings in boiling salted water, in an open pot, until done. When they bob up to the top of the water they are done and may be scooped out with a ladle. Drain them and place in a bowl.

Sprinkle with icing sugar and with the bread crumbs, which have been browned in a frying pan. Then sift icing sugar over them once more. You may make these with prune plums or damson plums, replacing the apricots with the plums.

Coconut Potato Kisses

Overall timing: 40 minutes   Makes: about 2 lbs.

1 cup	mashed dry-type potatoes	250 mL
2 tbsp.	softened butter	25 mL
1 lb.	confectioner's sugar	500 g
3 tbsp.	cocoa	45 mL
1 tsp.	vanilla	5 mL
½ tsp.	salt	2 mL
1 cup	coconut	250 mL

Prepare mashed potatoes, keep hot. Beat potatoes well to remove all lumps. Beat in butter, sugar, until thoroughly blended. Mix in cocoa, vanilla, salt, and coconut. If very stiff add more butter, up to 2 tbsp. (25 mL). Drop by teaspoonfuls on waxed paper. Let harden in refrigerator for a short time. Delicious.

*Variation:
— Omit cocoa, and dip kisses in 6 oz. (170 g) melted chocolate.

Chocolates with Grand Marnier

Overall timing: 40 minutes   Makes: 3 dozen

Fondant:

1 cup	raisins	250 mL
2 tbsp.	Grand Marnier	25 mL
1 tsp.	butter	5 mL
2 tbsp.	hot mashed boiling potatoes	25 mL
¼ cup	crushed, flaked, blanched almonds	50 mL
½ cup	coarsely chopped walnuts	125 mL
½ cup	icing sugar	125 mL
⅛ cup	potato flour	25 mL
2-2½ cups	icing sugar	500-625 mL

Dip:

6 oz.	semisweet baking chocolate	170 g

Chocolates with Grand Marnier (cont'd)

Soak raisins in Grand Marnier, 2 hours to overnight. Add butter to hot mashed potato. Stir in raisins, almonds, walnuts, and ½ cup (125 mL) icing sugar. Beat until all lumps are gone. Add potato flour, and 2 more cups (500 mL) icing sugar, or enough to make a mixture stiff enough to roll into rounds. Roll into walnut-sized rounds, place on waxed paper to dry slightly.

Melt 6 oz. (170 g) of semisweet baking chocolate in double boiler, over hot water. Melt slowly. Dip fruit-nut fondant in chocolate and place on waxed paper to set. Store in refrigerator.

Canadian and American pioneer women made candy out of mashed potatoes. This recipe is a twist on the old fashioned "pioneer candy".

Potato Peanut Butter Pioneer Candy

Overall timing: 3 hours   *Makes: 5 dozen pinwheels*

½ cup	cold, unseasoned mashed potatoes	125 mL
¼ cup	soft butter	50 mL
1 tsp.	vanilla	5 mL
4-5 cups	icing sugar, (more or less if needed)	1-1.25 L
1 cup	chunky style peanut butter	250 mL

Blend potatoes, butter and vanilla until smooth. Add icing sugar, one cup at a time, until dough is stiff enough to shape. "Caution" — Do not attempt to make this recipe in rainy or humid weather because candy will not harden properly. Roll candy out between 2 sheets of waxed paper into a rectangle, about 18" x 10" (44 x 25 cm) wide and ½" (1.3 cm) thick. Remove top piece of waxed paper, and spread with peanut butter. Roll up from the long side, jelly roll fashion. Cut roll into 2 rolls, and wrap each in waxed paper and chill 2 hours. To serve, cut rolls into ¼" thick slices. Keeps only a few days.

Petite Potato Chocolate Puffs

Overall timing: 35 minutes   Makes: 2 dozen

1¼ cups	cooked, cooled mashed potato (approx. 2 large potatoes)	300 mL
½ tsp.	baking powder	2 mL
⅛ cup	milk	25 mL
4 tbsp.	cocoa	60 mL
*2	squares semisweet chocolate bits	2
4 tbsp.	icing sugar	60 mL

Beat together all the ingredients, except chocolate pieces. Mixture should be fairly thick. Then stir in the chocolate pieces and drop by the teaspoonful (5 mL) into 375°F (190°C) fat. Fat must be very hot, so that the puffs are crisp almost immediately upon dropping into fat. Sprinkle with a delicate sprinkling of icing sugar and serve hot. May be reheated.

*You may substitute milk chocolate bar bits. A good way to utilize untouched chocolate Easter bunnies.

Russian Potato Pudding

Overall timing: 1 hour, 30 minutes   Serves: 6-8

5	medium baking potatoes, pared, finely grated	5
3	eggs, beaten	3
½ cup	brown sugar	125 mL
1 cup	cream	250 mL
1 tsp.	salt	5 mL
1 tbsp.	unbleached white flour	15 mL
1 tsp.	vanilla	5 ml
½ cup	unsweetened coconut	125 mL

Combine all ingredients except coconut, mix well. Place into a greased 3-quart (3 L) casserole. Sprinkle top with coconut. Bake at 450°F (230°C) for 15 minutes, then reduce heat to 350°F (180°C) and bake for another 45 minutes. Serve hot, with a dab of preserves.

Index

Index

Send *THE ORIGINAL INCREDIBLE POTATO* to a friend

The Original Incredible Potato is $16.95 per book plus $4.00 (total order) for shipping and handling.

Number of books _____ **x $16.95 = $** _____

Shipping and handling charge _____ **= $** **4.00**

Subtotal_____ **= $** _____

In Canada add 7% GST OR 15% HST where applicable _____ **= $** _____

Total enclosed _____ **= $** _____

$14.95 U.S. and international orders, payable in U.S. funds. U.S. shipping $4.00.
Price is subject to change.

NAME: _____

STREET:_____

CITY: _____ PROV./STATE _____

COUNTRY _____ POSTAL CODE/ZIP _____

Please make cheque or money order payable to: **ISIS Moon Publishing**
868 Drayton Street
FAX: 604-730-1004   **North Vancouver, BC**
E-mail: agnes_toews@hotmail.com   **Canada   V7L 2C4**

For fund raising or volume purchases,
contact **ISIS Moon Publishing** for volume rates.
Please allow 2-3 weeks for delivery.

....

Send *THE ORIGINAL INCREDIBLE POTATO* to a friend

The Original Incredible Potato is $16.95 per book plus $4.00 (total order) for shipping and handling.

Number of books _____ **x $16.95 = $** _____

Shipping and handling charge _____ **= $** **4.00**

Subtotal_____ **= $** _____

In Canada add 7% GST OR 15% HST where applicable _____ **= $** _____

Total enclosed _____ **= $** _____

$14.95 U.S. and international orders, payable in U.S. funds. U.S. shipping $4.00.
Price is subject to change.

NAME: _____

STREET:_____

CITY: _____ PROV./STATE _____

COUNTRY _____ POSTAL CODE/ZIP _____

Please make cheque or money order payable to: **ISIS Moon Publishing**
868 Drayton Street
FAX: 604-730-1004   **North Vancouver, BC**
E-mail: agnes_toews@hotmail.com   **Canada   V7L 2C4**

For fund raising or volume purchases,
contact **ISIS Moon Publishing** for volume rates.
Please allow 2-3 weeks for delivery.